The Complete Guide to
Patents®,
Copyrights©, and
Trademarks™

What You Need to Know Explained Simply

By Matthew L. Cole

THE COMPLETE GUIDE TO PATENTS, COPYRIGHTS, AND TRADEMARKS:
WHAT YOU NEED TO KNOW EXPLAINED SIMPLY

ISBN-13: 978-1-60138-231-3   ISBN-10: 1-60138-231-6

Library of Congress Cataloging-in-Publication Data

Cole, Matthew Lance, 1971-
  The complete guide to patents, copyrights, and trademarks : what you need to know explained simply / by Matthew L. Cole.
     p. cm.
  Includes bibliographical references and index.
  ISBN-13: 978-1-60138-231-3 (alk. paper)
  ISBN-10: 1-60138-231-6 (alk. paper)
  1. Intellectual property--United States. 2. Patent laws and legislation--United States. 3. Copyright--United States. 4. Trademarks--Law and legislation--United States. I. Title.
  KF2979.C65 2008
  346.7304'8--dc22
                              2008031626

INTERIOR LAYOUT DESIGN: Nicole Deck ndeck@atlantic-pub.com

Printed in the United States

We recently lost our beloved pet "Bear," who was not only our best and dearest friend but also the "Vice President of Sunshine" here at Atlantic Publishing. He did not receive a salary but worked tirelessly 24 hours a day to please his parents. Bear was a rescue dog that turned around and showered myself, my wife Sherri, his grandparents Jean, Bob and Nancy and every person and animal he met (maybe not rabbits) with friendship and love. He made a lot of people smile every day.

We wanted you to know that a portion of the profits of this book will be donated to The Humane Society of the United States.

–*Douglas & Sherri Brown*

THE HUMANE SOCIETY
OF THE UNITED STATES©

The human-animal bond is as old as human history. We cherish our animal companions for their unconditional affection and acceptance. We feel a thrill when we glimpse wild creatures in their natural habitat or in our own backyard.

Unfortunately, the human-animal bond has at times been weakened. Humans have exploited some animal species to the point of extinction.

The Humane Society of the United States makes a difference in the lives of animals here at home and worldwide. The HSUS is dedicated to creating a world where our relationship with animals is guided by compassion. We seek a truly humane society in which animals are respected for their intrinsic value, and where the human-animal bond is strong.

Want to help animals? We have plenty of suggestions. Adopt a pet from a local shelter, join The Humane Society and be a part of our work to help companion animals and wildlife. You will be funding our educational, legislative, investigative and outreach projects in the U.S. and across the globe.

Or perhaps you'd like to make a memorial donation in honor of a pet, friend or relative? You can through our Kindred Spirits program. And if you'd like to contribute in a more structured way, our Planned Giving Office has suggestions about estate planning, annuities, and even gifts of stock that avoid capital gains taxes.

Maybe you have land that you would like to preserve as a lasting habitat for wildlife. Our Wildlife Land Trust can help you. Perhaps the land you want to share is a backyard — that's enough. Our Urban Wildlife Sanctuary Program will show you how to create a habitat for your wild neighbors.

So you see, it's easy to help animals. And The HSUS is here to help.

The Humane Society of the United States
2100 L Street NW
Washington, DC 20037
202-452-1100
www.hsus.org

Dedication

For Mark Fleischman for allowing me to work on this at times when we were slow. Your patience, guidance, and friendship is, and will always be, appreciated.

Table of Contents

Introduction

"If nature has made any one thing less susceptible than all others of exclusive property, it is the action of the thinking power called an idea, which an individual may exclusively possess as long as he keeps it to himself; but the moment it is divulged, it forces itself into the possession of every one, and the receiver cannot dispossess himself of it."

Thomas Jefferson noting how intellectual property is different from other kinds of property in a letter to Isaac McPherson, Monticello, August 13, 1813

So you have written a novel, designed a new invention, or created a super logo to be the face of your company. Now what? You have taken the first step in ensuring that your ideas are protected: investing in this book protects inventions and logos. You will want to read the entire book since several areas overlap and because protecting your products, writing, and creations is good business. Copyrights, trademarks, and patents are considered intellectual property.

There are four fundamental forms of intellectual property that can be protected: patents, copyrights, trademarks, and trade secrets. Each form of intellectual property has a distinctive purpose in helping individuals and businesses protect their business assets. This book will explain the types of items that can be protected, the extent of the protection, the geographical areas where the protection extends, and the time the protection is made. This book is but one tool to be used on your path to copyright, patent, and trademark ownership.

Intellectual property law and policy are all about innovation, both encouraging it and protecting its fruits. However, these are potentially opposing, perhaps even incompatible, goals. If we reward one innovator with a monopoly over the fruits of the innovation, prohibiting others' use of those fruits, we risk preventing the next round of innovation. The challenge to lawmakers is to strike an appropriate balance between reward and innovation by pitching the length of the monopoly at the right level, both in the breadth of its coverage and the length of its term, beyond which others might also use it. Intellectual property ownership includes any work of authorship entitled to protection under the copyright laws.

The legal system grants definite rights and defense for owners of property. The kind of property that results from the hard work of writers, inventors, and companies is called intellectual property. Rights and protections for owners of intellectual property are based on federal patent, trademark and copyright laws, and state trade secret laws. In general, patents protect inventions of tangible things, copyrights protect a variety of forms of written and artistic expression, and trademarks protect a name or symbol that ascertain the source of goods or services.

Why should your intellectual property be copyrighted, patented, or trademarked? The answer is for the commercial value, which stems from your ability to control and exploit its use. If you were unable to reap the rewards of the ownership of your ideas, they would not bring you any wealth. If Walt Disney had not taken a chance by making a full-length animated motion picture in 1937, there would be no Disney® empire today. Despite being told that it was destined to fail, Disney made the feature film and, using copyright law, prevented others from taking his idea and reselling it. By using his ownership of the copyright of this film, he helped to create a monopoly on the animated film business for many years, ensuring the success of the Disney® empire of today.

The U.S. Constitutional Basis for Intellectual Property Protection, located in Article 1, Section 8, Clause 8, states: "The Congress shall have Power to promote the Progress of Science and useful Arts, by securing for limited Times to Authors and Inventors the exclusive Right to their respective Writings and Discoveries." It is interesting, however, to note that the U.S. Constitution was not specific in distinguishing copyrights from patents and put no exclusive limitations on either. The limitations would come later via the work of Thomas Jefferson, since he and James Madison corresponded as the Constitution and the Bill of Rights were being written. They saw the future problems that intellectual rights could create if they were not addressed then.

Alexander Wolcott received the first American patent for his camera in 1840.

Chapter 1

Intellectual Property Protection

"Imagination is more important than knowledge."

Albert Einstein

Although intellectual property does share some of the same characteristics as real estate and personal property, note that each are considered assets and can be bought, sold, exchanged, licensed, and given away like other forms of property. Intellectual property owners thus have the right to prevent the unauthorized use or sale of their property. The most glaring and obvious differences between other forms of property and intellectual property are that the latter is intangible. That means it is not defined or recognized by physical factors of its own. Intellectual property must be expressed in some noticeable way in order to ensure protection for it.

Creating a Personal Plan

After reading this book, start taking notes on the legal steps to ensure your writing, creation, or invention is protected fully under current laws. This is known as your personal plan. This plan will include what you can expect to gain by knowledge and protection for your intellectual property. You can then apply your plan to the correct organizations, using the proper forms and getting them to the right people. This ensures that your intellectual property is safe and protected, so your business or ideas can start making you money.

One or more of the three types of intellectual property protection discussed in this book may protect a product: copyrights, patents, or trademarks. A common example is a household lamp with a sculptured base. A patent may protect the practical electric components of the lamp and the light bulb. The label on the lamp may hold a trademark recognizing the source of the lamp that differentiates it from other manufacturers' lamps. The sculptured lamp base may be considered a work of art and consequently be subject to copyright protection. Ultimately, the manufacturer may have amassed a list of customers who are known to buy such lamps or a list of preferred parts suppliers. If these lists have been kept confidential and secret, they may be trade secrets.

> To promote the Progress of Science and useful Arts, by securing for limited Times to Authors and Inventors the exclusive Right to their respective Writings and Discoveries

Patents, trademarks, copyrights, and trade secrets have an independent value as a business asset. This value may be actively used for commercial gain. Because an owner of intellectual property has exclusive rights in that property, the owner may permit others to use the property for a fee. Such licensing arrangements are quite common and profitable. Cross licensing is another technique used by companies to profit from their intellectual property portfolios.

Setting Up Your Protection

Intellectual property is protected on a national basis. The particular scope of protection and the requirements for obtaining protection will fluctuate from country to country. There are, however, comparisons among national legal arrangements. Moreover, the current worldwide trend is toward balancing the national laws. The countries that grant for the protection of intellectual property benefit in many ways, like increasing the general pool of information and knowledge and because adequate legal protection fosters investment and trade. When looking for new markets or countries in which to expand manufacturing or distribution facilities, companies often look to countries that will protect their intellectual property.

The exclusive rights granted to the copyright owner do not include the right to prevent others from making fair use of the owner's work. Such fair use may include use of the work for purposes of criticism, comment, news reporting, teaching or education, scholarship, or research. The nature of the work, the extent of the work copied, and the impact of copying on the work's commercial value are all considered in determining whether an unauthorized use is a "fair use."

In order to obtain rights and protection for your works, several factors must be met. This includes originality of the work, which ensures the work of authorship came from the author and was not copied from other works. Then the works must contain originality in sufficient amount to prove they are more than variations of pre-existing works.

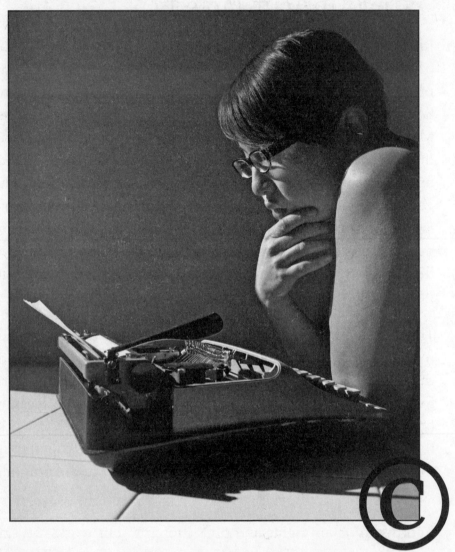

Filing a copyright on a literary work is easy. All you need to do is send an application, a copy of the work, and a check to the U.S. copyright office.

Chapter 2

Copyrights at a Glance

"The way to get started is to quit talking and begin doing."

Walt Disney

Copyright occurs automatically when two conditions are satisfied: the creation of an original work and the fixation of that work in any tangible medium of expression. It was formerly assumed that whoever wrote a book or article, thus creating it, was the copyright owner. This is not necessarily the case. Numerous writers and artists have made this mistake and have paid for it dearly. Do not make the same mistake. Just because you create an original piece of work, you do not automatically take ownership of the copyright. There are exceptions to every rule.

For example, look at the copyright of this book. Although I am the author, I am not the copyright holder of this original work. This is an example of a work-for-hire copyright situation. Other potential exceptions occur when the work has been produced as a work for hire, if independent contractors hire the creator, or if you are an employee and create the work through the course of your employment. It is always best to do your homework and make sure if you create something, you know your rights and limitations regarding that piece of work.

You may have written a novel or a children's book or you may want to publish your family history in book form. These projects take time and effort on your part, so be sure to protect your rights.

Why Should I Copyright?

Brad Templeton answers this on his Web site, found at **www. templetons.com**, noting that "Copyright law secures for the creator of a creative effort the exclusive right to control who can make copies, or make works derived from the original work. There are a lot of subtleties and international variations, but that is the gist of it. If you create something, and it fits the definition of a creative work, you get to control who can make copies of it and how they make copies, with some important exceptions. You can also sell or license this right, or if you do the work for somebody who hired you to do it, they buy this right in advance."

Still not sure if your project qualifies for copyright protection, and wondering who can claim copyright? Keep reading — the answers to your questions await you.

Copyright protection subsists from the time the work is fashioned in unchanging form. Think of a bound and printed book. The copyright in the work of authorship instantaneously becomes the property of the author who created the work. Note only the author or those deriving their rights through the author can rightfully claim copyright.

As in the case of this book, the individual deriving the rights is the publisher. Because it is a work-for-hire arrangement, the employer (or publisher) and not the employee (the actual writer) is considered to be the author. The United States Copyright Office lists Section 101 of the copyright law defines a "work made-for-hire" as:

A work prepared by an employee within the scope of his or her employment; or a work specially ordered or commissioned for use as:

- A contribution to a collective work

- A part of a motion picture or other audiovisual work

- A translation

- A supplementary work

- A compilation

- An instructional text

- An answer for a test

- An atlas

The authors of a joint work are co-owners of the copyright in the work, except if there is an understanding to the contrary. Copyright in each individual contribution to a periodical or other shared work is dissimilar from copyright in the combined work as a whole and rests initially with the author of the contribution. Copyright protection is available for all unpublished works, in spite of the nationality or residence of the author.

Okay, so do you still want to know what type of protection you will receive from copyrighting your material?

A work that was created or fixed in a real or tangible form for the first time, on or after January 1, 1978, is automatically protected from the moment of its creation and is usually given a term lasting for the author's life in addition to 70 years after the author's death. In the case of "a joint work prepared by two or more authors who did not work for hire," the term lasts for 70 years after the last surviving author's death. For works made-for-hire, and for anonymous and pseudonymous works, the length of copyright will be 95 years from publication or 120 years from creation, whichever is shorter.

Pseudonyms are when you use a pen or fictitious name. Anonymous is when the author is not known, unless the author's identity is revealed in United States Copyright Office records and asked to be kept secret.

Works initially created before January 1, 1978, although not published or registered by that date, have been automatically brought under the statute and are given federal copyright protection. The duration of copyright in these works is computed in the same way as for works created on or after January 1, 1978: the life-plus-70 or 95/120-year terms relate to them as well. The law affords that in no case would the term of copyright for works in this category end before December 31, 2002, and for works published on or before December 31, 2002, the term of copyright will not expire before December 31, 2047.

Overview of Copyright

Some people confuse patents, copyrights, and trademarks. Although there may be some parallels among these kinds of intellectual property protection, they are different and serve different purposes. However, the differences are simple.

Copyright is a form of protection provided to the authors of "original works of authorship."

As stated by the United States Copyright Office, copyright is a form of protection provided by the laws of the United States for original works of authorship, including literary, dramatic, musical, architectural, cartographic, choreographic, pantomimic, pictorial, graphic, sculptural, and audiovisual creations. "Copyright" literally means the right to copy. It is legal to produce alternate versions of a copyrighted work to provide improved access to work for blind and visually impaired persons without permission from the copyright holder.

Copyright laws, along with several court decisions and regulations, have established rules governing the following activities: licensing and selling of intellectual property; the resolution of disputes between companies and individuals for creating or selling similar intellectual property, products and/ or services; and the administration and registration of intellectual property. Intellectual property can refer to products of the human mind that produce a commercial value. Typically, this encompasses creative works, products, imagery, services, inventions, or processes. Copyright laws have been set up to protect these activities by patent, trademark, or copyright. As far as the United States Copyright Office is concerned, copyright protection does not extend to any idea, procedure, process, slogan, principle, or discovery.

Who Can Claim Copyright?

From the time a work is created in fixed form, copyright protection exists. The author who created it instantly obtains the copyright and this becomes their property. The author is the only one who can lawfully claim copyright after obtaining their rights.

What Rights Does the Owner Have?

Within the period of copyright, the creator has specific exclusive rights to communicate, copy, or publish their work. These rights can be assigned or varied by contract. Where the ownership of copyright has been contractually varied, the copyright owner, as opposed to the original author, owns the copyright.

In a July 31, 1788 letter from Thomas Jefferson — you will see he was using codes to hide his content from spies — "this statement was in a letter to Madison after the above one that is purported to be saying Jefferson wants no monopoly" (Thibadeau, Robert).

Below is the content and a photo of the actual letter, courtesy of Central Michigan University:

"I sincerely rejoice at the acceptance of our new constitution by nine states. It is a good canvas, on which some strokes only want retouching. What these are, I think are sufficiently manifested by the general voice from North to South, which calls for a bill of rights. It seems pretty generally understood that this should go to Juries, Habeas corpus, Standing armies, Printing, Religion and Monopolies. I conceive there may be difficulty in finding general modification of these suited to the habits of all the states. But if such cannot be found then it is better to establish trials by jury, the right of Habeas corpus, freedom of the press and freedom of religion in all cases, and to abolish standing armies in time of peace, and Monopolies, in all cases, than not to do it in any. The few cases wherein these things may do evil, cannot be weighed against the multitude wherein the want of them will do evil. In disputes between a foreigner and a native, a trial by jury may be improper. But if this exception cannot be agreed to, the remedy will be to model the jury by giving the medietas linguae *in civil as well as criminal cases. Why suspend the Hab. corp. in insurrections and rebellions? The parties who may be arrested may be charged instantly*

with a well-defined crime. Of course the judge will remand them. If the public safety requires that the government should have a man imprisoned on less probable testimony in those than in other emergencies; let him be taken and tried, retaken and retried, while the necessity continues, only giving him redress against the government for damages. Examine the history of England: see how few of the cases of the suspension of the Habeas corpus law have been worthy of that suspension. They have been either real treasons wherein the parties might as well have been charged at once, or sham-plots where it was shameful they should ever have been suspected. Yet for the few cases wherein the suspension of the hab. corp. has done real good, that operation is now become habitual, and the minds of the nation almost prepared to live under its constant suspension. A declaration that the federal government will never restrain the presses from printing anything they please, will not take away the liability of the printers for false facts printed. The declaration that religious faith shall be unpunished, does not give impunity to criminal acts dictated by religious error. The saying there shall be no monopolies lessens the incitements to ingenuity, which is spurred on by the hope of a monopoly for a limited time, as of 14 years; but the benefit even of limited monopolies is too doubtful to be opposed to that of their general suppression. If no check can be found to keep the number of standing troops within safe bounds, while they are tolerated as far as necessary, abandon them altogether, discipline well the militia, and guard the magazines with them. More than magazine-guards will be useless if few, and dangerous if many. No European nation can ever send against us such a regular army as we need fear, and it is hard if our militias are not equal to those of Canada or Florida. My idea then is, that tho' proper exceptions to these general rules are desirable and probably practicable, yet if the exceptions cannot be agreed on, the establishment of the roles in all cases will do ill in very few. I hope therefore a bill of rights will be formed to guard the people against the federal government, as they are already guarded against their state governments in most instances."

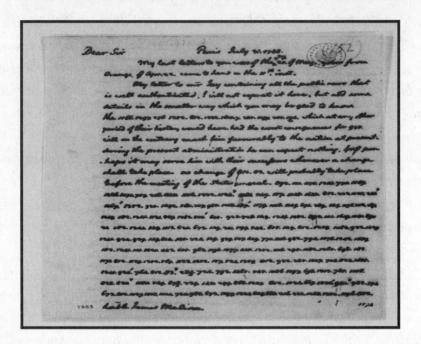

Copyright Rights, Unregulated Uses, and Fair Use

In this drawing, Erik J. Heels attempt to explain the wonderful world of copyright law. Heels thinks all intellectual property lawyers (i.e. patent, trademark, copyright, and trade secret) enjoy writing about copyright.

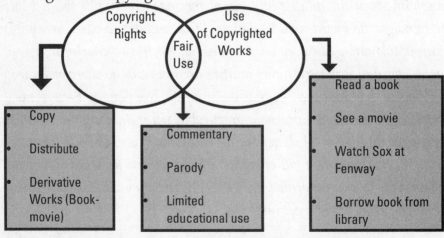

Everyone is familiar with what copyright protects — books, movies, CDs, DVDs, radio, TV, etc. — even if they do not practice copyright law. What most people do not know is that there are three types of uses of copyrighted material, and not all of those rights are protected (and hence can be legally controlled) by the copyright owner.

Have you ever seen a copyright notice that says, "It is illegal to make a copy of this copyrighted document"? That is not entirely true, because it excludes fair use. Heels often thought the Copyright Act should be amended to say that all copyrights are forfeited if an incorrect copyright notice is placed on a work. However, the likelihood of that happening is slim.

On the right side of the drawing are unregulated uses — those not covered by copyright rights. You do not need permission from the copyright owner to:

- Read a book

- See a movie

- Watch the Red Sox at Fenway Park

- Borrow a book from a library

In the middle of the drawing are uses that are covered by copyright but have been declared to be "fair use" by the law. You can use copyrighted works without permission (to some extent) for:

- Commentary

- Parody

- Limited educational use

On the left side of the drawing are the exclusive uses for copyright owners. These include the rights to:

- Copy the work

- Distribute the work

- Make derivative works from the work (such as making a movie from a book)

To sum up, there are three classes of copyright uses: unregulated, fair, and protected. You need to think carefully about which type of use you require. Unfortunately, many copyright owners fail to do this.

*Drawing That Explains Copyright Law by Erik J. Heels, MIT engineer, patent and trademark lawyer, **(http://www.erikjheels.com)**.*

Copyright History

The history of copyrights in the United States is unique and varied. Our first glimpse into copyright comes from the Constitution. "The historical records around these quotes reveal quite a lot, but I find it is hard to get perfectly clearly into the mind of Thomas Jefferson on this and perfectly clearly into the role that Jefferson had in that line in the Constitution … Some people have noted Jefferson was in France while the U.S. Constitution was written. So, he could not have been seminally involved in establishing what has become the world standard for Intellectual Property." (Thibadeau, Robert) It can also be argued that Thomas Jefferson was an integral part of the construction of the Constitution, especially after James Madison, as a definer and procreator of intellectual property rights, wrote it, as we know them today.

To fully comprehend copyright, studying the history of it helps in explaining the need, the protection and why it is important. The United States Copyright Office offers this brief history of copyrighting in the United States: The Constitution gives Congress the power to enact laws establishing a system of copyright in the United States. Congress enacted the first federal copyright law in May 1790, and the first work was registered within two weeks. In his article "A Brief History of Copyright Law," George Johnson notes, "Authors, patrons, and owners of works throughout the ages have tried to direct and control how copies of such works could be used once disseminated to others."

Originally, clerks of U.S. District Courts recorded claims. It was not until 1870 that copyright functions were centralized in the Library of Congress under the direction of the then-Librarian of Congress, Ainsworth Rand Spoofed. The Copyright Office became a separate department of the Library of Congress in 1897, and Thorvald Solberg was appointed the first Register of Copyrights. The United States Copyright Office of today is one of the major service units of the Library of Congress, occupying portions of the James Madison Memorial Building. The great repository known as the Library of Congress houses more than 126 million items and has greatly enhanced the operations of the copyright system.

A Timeline of Copyright

1790 — The first U.S. Copyright Act is created by George Washington and enacted by Congress. It gave authors of books, maps, and charts ownership of their work for up to 28 years.

1831 — Congress includes musical pieces in the Copyright Act.

1841 — "Fair Use Doctrine" is born in Massachusetts after the Folsom v. Marsh decision ruled that an author had the right to use letters George Washington wrote to a friend as the basis for a new work.

1908 — Supreme Court rules in favor of White-Smith Music Publishing Company against Apollo Co., maker of player piano scrolls, opining that piano scrolls were not copies and therefore did not infringe.

1909 — Congress amends the Copyright Act to include new technologies like piano rolls and sound recordings.

1975 — Sony introduces the Betamax home videocassette recorder. Several companies, including Disney and Universal, sue Sony because the new product makes it easy to copy protected works. The Supreme Court rules in favor of Sony, opining that the machines could be used for non-infringing uses like time shifting or recording to watch at another time.

1976 — Congress amends the Copyright Act, which, among other things, addresses issues created by new information storage, retrieval, reproduction, and display technology, and formalizes the fair use doctrine by laying out a four-part standard for determining fair use.

1990 — Architectural works become subject to copyright law.

1998 — Congress enacts the Sonny Bono Copyright Term Extension Act. The act expands copyright limits by 20 years on existing and future works. Currently, copyrighted works are protected for the author's life plus 70 years.

1998 — Congress enacts the Digital Millennium Copyright Act (DMCA), which regulates many issues related to digital storage, retrieval, reproduction, and display of copyrighted material.

2000 — The Children's Internet Protection Act (CIPA) is signed into law. CIPA requires all schools and libraries that receive specific federal funds to have in place an Internet Safety Policy which uses Internet filtering technology to block access to obscenity, child pornography, or material harmful to minors.

2002 — A panel of federal judges finds the CIPA is unconstitutional. The federal government subsequently appeals the decision to the Supreme Court.

2005 — The Family Entertainment and Copyright Act is enacted.

Comparative Copyright Laws

Copyrights can be established for original or new expressions created by composers, musicians, authors, artists, designers, and other creative individuals. Simple ownership of a book, manuscript, painting, or any other copy or phono-record does not give the owner the copyright. The law allows that transfer of ownership of any material object that demonstrates a protected work does not of itself articulate any rights in the copyright.

Minors may assert copyright, but state laws may regulate the business dealings concerning copyrights owned by minors. For information on relevant state laws, consult an attorney. Copyright is only one type of intellectual property law. It was created to protect the works of authorship, computer software, and architecture. However, you cannot copyright facts, systems, and methods of operation, ideas, or the way in which things are expressed.

Copyright laws are aimed at protecting the creators of intellectual property, but there are many things not protected by copyright law. Under the copyright laws, domain names are not protected. There are ways to ensure protection for them by accessing the Internet Corporation for Assigned Names and Numbers. This nonprofit organization administers domain name system management.

Copyright law also does not protect slogans, names, or short phrases. In a few select cases these things may be protected as trademarks. When unsure, it is always best to check with the United States Copyright Office or a copyright attorney before using one of these.

The United States Copyright Act grants certain exclusive rights to the owner of a copyright in a work. These exclusive rights are different from the rights given to a person who merely owns a copy of the work.

For example, when a person purchases a book at a bookstore, they have received a property right in a copy of a copyrighted work (i.e. the book). The book's owner may then resell the book, or even destroy it, since they own the book. However, the book's owner did not receive any copyrights when purchasing the book.

The book's author holds all copyrights until the author specifically transfers them. Consequently, the book owner may not make any copies of the book, since the right to copy a work is one of the exclusive rights granted under the Copyright Act. This distinction allows a copyright owner to sell copies of a work, or even the original work itself, such as a sculpture, without forfeiting rights under the Copyright Act.

Chapter 3

Copyright Categories

"Only one thing is impossible for God: to find any sense in any copyright law on the planet . . . Whenever a copyright law is to be made or altered, then the idiots assemble."

Mark Twain

First we will cover all the copyright categories and how they differ legally. Choose the appropriate one for your work and set up various other protection measures.

Literary Works

One of the most significant legal concepts that any writer must become intimate with is United States copyright law. Copyright law protects "works of authorship," which include literary works such as short fiction, short stories, novels, nonfiction articles, poetry, newspaper articles, newspapers, magazine articles, magazines, computer software, software manuals, text advertisements, manuals, catalogs, brochures, and compilations of information such as databases.

Publication has a technical connotation in copyright law. According to U.S. Copyright statute, "Publication is the distribution of copies or phono-records of a work to the public by sale or other transfer of ownership, or by rental, lease, or lending. The offering to distribute copies or phono-records to a group of persons for purposes of further distribution, public performance, or public display constitutes publication. A public performance or display of a work does not of itself constitute publication."

Why should you register your work with the United States Copyright Office? There are several reasons to register. For one, to sue someone for copyright infringement, the owner of the work must first register the work with the U.S. Copyright Office. You may register the work after someone has infringed upon the work, but the registration will only be relevant to infringements that occur after the registration. On the other hand, if you register your work within 90 days of publication, the statutory damages provisions apply to infringements before and after the tangible registration. Registered works may be eligible for statutory damages up to $100,000 and attorney's fees in successful litigation. If the registration is completed within five years from the creation of the work, it is considered prima facie proof in a court of law.

Registration is inexpensive, about $20 per work registered, and relatively straightforward. To register, the author simply fills out the copyright application and mails it to the U.S. Copyright office with a check and a non-returnable copy of the work (one copy if the work is unpublished, two copies if it has been published). Pieces of published works have to be registered within three months of the publication. This is called "mandatory deposit."

The United States Copyright Office has issued a Notice of

Proposed Rulemaking, which will modify the way it accepts group registrations of individual works. The proposed change would affect writers of short works, which they group and register collectively; it also would require electronic registration.

This was taken from the National Registry:

NOTICE OF PROPOSED RULEMAKING
LIBRARY OF CONGRESS
Copyright Office
Registration of Claims to Copyright, Group Registration Options

AGENCY: Copyright Office, Library of Congress

ACTION: Notice of Proposed Rulemaking.

SUMMARY OF THE CHANGES:

The Copyright Office of the Library of Congress is proposing to amend its regulations governing the registration options, which allow grouping of individual works to be registered using one application to require online submission for these options.

PURPOSE THIS IS TO ADDRESS:

If hand-delivered by a private party, an original and five copies of the comments should be brought to Room 401 of the James Madison Building between 8:30 a.m. and 5 p.m.

The material should be addressed as follows:

Office of the General Counsel, Library of Congress, James Madison Building, LM-401, Washington, D.C. 20559-6000.

If delivered by a commercial courier, an original and five copies must be delivered to the Congressional Courier Acceptance Site (CCAS) located at:

2nd and D Streets, NE, Washington, D.C. 20559

Hours are between 8:30 a.m. and 4 p.m.

NOTICE OF PROPOSED RULEMAKING

The envelope should be addressed as follows:

Office of the General Counsel
U.S. Copyright Office, LM 401
James Madison Building,
101 Independence Avenue, SE
Washington, D.C.

Please note that CCAS will not accept delivery by means of overnight delivery services such as Federal Express, United Parcel Service, or DHL.

Background of Copyright

When Congress ratified its major revision to the copyright law in 1976, it provided for a solitary registration for a group of related works and explained in the legislative history the need for allowing registration options in which a group of related works might be registered together. Congress pointed out the "unnecessary burdens and expenses" connected with requiring separate registrations (including multiple sets of application forms and multiple fees) for separate works. Congress even gave examples where a single registration might be made rather than multiple registrations, including the various editions or issues of a daily newspaper.

To accommodate this need, the register has issued regulations offering a group registration option in which published, related individual works of authorship may be combined and presented for registration for one fee, using one application form, and sending one group of required deposit copies. The group registration option may be used to register a group of serial issues first published on or after January 7, 1991, at intervals of a week or longer within a three-month period during the same calendar year; a group of newspapers published within the same month; a group of newsletter issues first published on or after July 1, 1999, with the claim including two or more issues within a single calendar month within the same calendar year; a group of contributions to a periodical, including a newspaper, by the same individual author; a group of published photographs by the same photographer, whether the author is an individual or an employer for hire, first published in the same calendar year; and a group of updates or revisions to a database, added over a period of time, whether or not they are published.

Shared Worlds or Universes

A shared world or universe is a literary technique in which several different authors create works of fiction that share aspects such as settings or characters and that are intended to be read as taking place in a single universe. This can be contrasted with collaborative writing, in which multiple authors work on a single story. Shared universes are more common within fantasy and science fiction than in other genres.

There is no formalized definition of when the appearance of fictional characters in another author's work constitutes a shared universe. Fiction in some media, such as most television programs and many comic book titles, is understood to require the contribution of multiple authors and does not by itself create a shared universe. Incidental appearances, such as that of d'Artagnan in *Cyrano de Bergerac*, may instead be considered literary cameos.

The modern definition of copyright, especially under United States copyright law, considers the expansion of a previous work's setting or characters to be a derivative work. Especially for material being considered for publication, this often necessitates licensing agreements. For this reason, some fan fiction and other amateur works written in established settings without permission are sometimes distinguished from shared universe writings or even described as a "stolen universe." However, fair use claims have been raised, and not all authors believe that fan fiction should be distinguished from other literature in this manner at all.

In a process similar to brand licensing, the intellectual property owners of established fictional settings at times allow others to author new material, creating an expanded universe. Such franchises, generally based on television programs or film, allow for series of novels, video games, original sound recordings, and other media. Not all shared universe settings are simply the expansion or combination of pre-existing material by new authors. At times, an author or group of authors has created a setting specifically for development by multiple authors, often through collaboration.

Note: Be sure to check with the copyright office to see which category your work falls under.

Musical Works

Songwriters should always copyright their work as soon as completed as often musicians mistake copyrighting and the registering of music as the same entity. To ensure that you will have protection, always write the copyright information on your demos, lyric sheet, music score, CDs or any other recorded material cover in this format:

© Date, Name. All songs are copyright-controlled. The copyright in these sound recordings is owned by [Name]. All Rights Reserved.

This should be done previously to sealing all works in an envelope, which should be signed and dated across the seal. Copyrighting and registering music are separate. Copyright law automatically protects works written or recorded in a permanent form.

A musical work is any musical composition. This is not an actual recording of something that would be an audiovisual or sound work. The author of a musical work is the musician who composes the music and writes the lyrics. Generally, for a compact disc (CD) there are two copyrights for every song — one for the musical work and one for the actual sound recording on the disc. You will need to protect your masterpiece and provide proof of ownership in case of future dispute. If there is more than one songwriter they each should agree to a contribution split and sign a confirmation of agreement.

The copyright laws permit registration of sound recordings. Only sound recordings that have been "fixed" may be protected under copyright laws. In other words, a work must be "recorded by any method now known or later developed" in order to receive protection.

There are three aspects of musical works that must be separately considered under the copyright laws. The first aspect is the sound recording itself. The sound recording embodies the actual sound of the music. The second is the visual transcription of the words and music involved in the musical work (i.e. the lyrics and sheet music). The third aspect is musical sound that is part of a motion picture or audiovisual work.

When a musical work is incorporated with a motion picture or audiovisual work, the musical aspects of the movie are protected as part of the copyright on the motion picture itself. The musical features of a sound recording are generally registered separately from the transcription. Separate forms are used to register these two components of the musical work. It is possible, however, to register the sound recording and transcription of the music together on a single application. This requires yet a different form. Combined registration can only be made if the claimant of both aspects of the musical work is the same.

Music can be protected well before the publication or release of the songs to protect your rights as a musician or creator.

Dramatic Works

The United States Copyright Offices maintains dramatic works such as plays and radio or television scripts are works intended to be performed. Dramatic works usually include spoken text, plot, and directions for action. The types of published or unpublished dramatic works that may be submitted for registration include choreography, pantomimes, plays, treatments, and scripts prepared for cinema, radio, and television. These works may be with or without music.

Copyright law does not explicitly define what qualifies as a dramatic work. However, it is generally understood that dramatic works include all performed actions, speeches, dramas, etc., which convey information to an audience.

Because of misconceptions about copyright registration for radio and television presentations, the following points require emphasis:

- The title of a program or series of programs cannot be copyrighted.

- The general idea or concept for a program is not copyrightable. Copyright will protect the literary or dramatic expression of an author's idea but not the idea itself.

- Registration for a particular script applies only to the copyrightable material in that script; blanket registration for future scripts or for a series as a whole is not available.

Choreographic Works

Choreography is the art of making structures in which movement occurs. People who create choreography are called choreographers. The United States Copyright Office states that choreography and pantomime are also copyrightable dramatic works. Choreography is the composition and arrangement of dance movements and patterns usually intended to be accompanied by music.

Copyright law does not explicitly define what a pantomime or choreographic work is, but this category is generally understood to include dance routines, ballet, gymnastic floor routines, etc.

As distinct from choreography, pantomime is the art of imitating or acting out situations, characters, or other events. To be protected by copyright, pantomimes and choreography need not tell a story or be presented before an audience. Each work, however, must be fixed in a tangible medium of expression from which the work can be performed (United States Copyright Office).

Since January 1, 1978, choreographic works have been available to copyright laws and protection. Prior to the effective date of the Federal Copyright Law of 1976, most of the choreographic works were offered protection under the category of dramatic and musical works.

Choreographic work is not defined in the 1976 statute, although the legislative history offers some minimal guidance. The House and Senate Reports use identical language to say that the term is one of several with fairly settled meanings, and that it is not "necessary to specify that 'choreographic works' do not include social dance steps and simple routines" [S. Rep. No. 473, 94th Cong., 1st Session 52 (1975); H.R. Rep. No. 1476, 94th Cong., 2nd Session 53-54 (1976)]. These reports, typically issued after hearings on proposed legislation, are enormously important in determining Congressional intent, when the language of the statute is not clear and complete in itself.

Audiovisual & Sound Works

The United States Copyright Office states that copyright of a sound recording protects the particular series of sounds that are fixed or embodied in a recording against unauthorized reproduction and revision, unauthorized distribution of phono-records containing those sounds, and certain unauthorized performances by means of a digital audio transmission. The Digital Performance Right in Sound Recordings Act of 1995, P.L. 104-39, effective February 1, 1996, created a new limited performance right for certain digital transmissions of sound recordings. Generally, copyright protection extends to two elements in a sound recording: the performance, and the production or engineering of the sound recording.

Copyright law defines an audiovisual work as a series of associated images, which are capable of being shown by some device, such as a projector, along with any sounds, which go together with the visual portion of the work.

In order to qualify as a motion picture or audiovisual work, the work must have a visual component, although it need not have an audio component. Therefore, a silent movie qualifies, but a movie soundtrack does not.

Architectural Works

Architectural work became subject matter to copyright protection on December 1, 1990. Copyright law defines it as "the design of a building embodied in any tangible medium of expression, including a building, drawings or architectural plans."

Any architectural work created on or after December 1, 1990 was extended copyright protection. Incomplete works or works that remained in unpublished plans or drawings on that date were also given unmitigated protection. Works prior to this date were not granted copyright protection under the current laws.

Compilations

The United States Copyright Office defines a compilation as a work, which is the collection and assembly of other pre-existing materials, which are selected and arranged in such a way that the final work is an original work of authorship.

The most frequent type of compilation is a collected work, which is defined by the Copyright Act as a periodical, anthology or encyclopedia which uses pre-existing materials that were protected works on their own, and accumulated them into a single work. A compilation is not free to any independent copyright protection if the author of the compilation did not obtain the obligatory permission to use the underlying and pre-existing materials.

Derivative Works

Copyright laws define a derivative work as any work established from one or more pre-existing works. This includes translations, dramatizations, movie adaptations, abridgments, and any form of transformation or adaptation. Examples of a derivative work would include the film version *Harry Potter and the Sorcerer's Stone*, adapting the book; an English translation of a foreign language novel; or a drawing based on a photograph.

If the author of the derivative work had the permission of the original author to use the original work, or if the original work was in the public domain, then the derivative work can be copyrighted on its own. This brings into question such areas as public domain and ghostwriting.

Ghostwriting is when a professional writer is paid to write books, articles, stories, reports, or other materials that are officially credited to another person, though the author or publisher for their assistance sometimes acknowledges ghostwriters. Ghostwriters are hired for numerous reasons. In countless cases, celebrities or public figures do not have the time, discipline, or writing skills to write and do research for an autobiography or "how-to" book of several hundred pages.

Even when celebrities or public figures have the writing talent to pen a short article, they may not know how to structure and edit a several-hundred page book so it is enchanting and well paced. In other cases, publishers use ghostwriters to augment the number of books that can be published each year under the name of well-known, marketable authors. Ghostwriters often spend from several months to a full year researching, writing, and editing non-fiction works for their clients, and are paid either per page, with a flat fee, or a percentage of the royalties of the sales.

Celebrities and public figures that wish to publish their autobiographies or memoirs extensively use ghostwriters. The degree of participation of the ghostwriter in non-fiction writing projects ranges from minor to considerable. In some cases, a ghostwriter may be called in just to clean up, edit, and polish a rough draft of an autobiography.

The right to make a derivative work overlaps somewhat with the reproduction right. According to the Copyright Act, a derivative work is a work based on one or more pre-existing works, such as a translation, musical arrangement, dramatization, fictionalization, motion picture version, sound recording, art reproduction, abridgment, condensation, or any other form in which a work may be recast, transformed, or adapted.

Pictorial, Graphic, and Sculptural Works

Copyright law broadly defines pictorial, graphic, and sculptural works as including all two-dimensional and three-dimensional works of art (fine art, graphic art, and applied art), photographs, prints, reproductions, maps, globes, charts, diagrams, models, and technical drawings, including architectural plans.

This can encompass everything from sculptures and paintings to less conventional items like mannequins and decorative belt buckles. And as with other works of art, the required level of creativity is minimal, so this also includes everything from realistic photographs to drawings and renditions of a product.

Electronic Works

Copyright and the Internet

The emergence of the Internet has made the infringement of copyright works simpler and harder to hunt down. Whether of a major film, recorded song, software package, electronically published report, or personal travel photo, illegal copying or piracy is made far easier by digital technology. Originators should seek professional advice on protecting their work.

Some experts feel the intellectual property situation in regard to the Internet is getting to its worst point ever, as this area requires knowledge of technology and law. The Internet has created even more copyright problems. When an author places his or her work on a home page, it can be viewed by people all around the world, in countries which have no copyright treaty with the United States. Even if the author's work is infringed upon, he or she may never even be informed about it if the work is reproduced in a foreign country. Additionally, it is costly to pursue a copyright violation lawsuit in a foreign country.

What do I do if I discover my work has been infringed upon from the Internet?

If you find a copyright violation, the first step is to write a letter to the offending party asking that the infringing information be removed from the Web site. If the infringing material is found on a Web site and the owner declines to remove the offending material, you may consider reporting to the owner's Internet

Service Provider (ISP) about the circumstances. The law in several countries is changing to hold ISPs liable for violations of a variety of laws by users of the ISP, and many ISPs will take action about complaints in regards to illegal activities on members' Web sites.

Serial or Periodical Works

For copyright purposes, serials are defined as works issued or intended to be issued in successive parts bearing numerical or chronological designations and intended to be continued indefinitely.

Examples of serial works are periodicals, newspapers, magazines, bulletins, newsletters, annuals, journals, or proceedings of societies.

The following information from the United States Copyright Office will help you understand and prepare your application for copyright protection. Be sure to read carefully, since missing even the smallest of details could delay or jeopardize the status of your right to ownership.

Making Sure Your Application Is Acceptable

In order to make sure your application will be acceptable, give clear and accurate information.

In completing an application form to register a request to copyright, it is important to give clear and accurate information. To make certain the information is correct, read the instructions on the application form meticulously. Additional information on an assortment of topics is available from the Copyright Office if required. See "For Further Information" below.

Type or complete the application in black ink.

It is also vital that the information you give in your application is dark enough to make an acceptable copy. The registration certificate issued by the Copyright Office is made from a photographic image of your application. The better the quality of your application, the better the quality of your certificate will be. Applications of tremendously inferior quality will not be accepted. In completing your application form, use a typewriter or printer with a good ribbon, or clearly print all information, except your signature, with a pen in black ink. Do not use a pencil or colored pens (blue, green, red, etc.).

Only use acceptable photocopies or computer printouts of copyright office forms.

If you use a printed form issued by the Copyright Office, you do not have to worry about the quality of the form itself; it will produce an acceptable certificate. Then again, the Copyright Office receives applications in an assortment of paper formats in addition to the printed application forms it distributes. These include:

- Photocopies of Copyright Office-issued forms

- Printed paper copies of forms from the Copyright Office Web site at **www.copyright.gov/forms**

- Printed paper copies of other computer-produced Copyright Office forms that have been approved by the Copyright Office

If the application you use is a photocopy or a computer printout, make sure it is clear, legible, and on high-quality 8 ½ x 11" white paper. Also make sure the form meets the following criteria:

The two-page form must be printed head to head on a single sheet of paper so that when you turn the sheet over, the top of page 2 is directly behind the top of page 1.

Do not enlarge or reduce the size of the form. The top and bottom margins of the form must be the same as those on the printed form issued by the Copyright Office. In particular, the return address at the bottom of page 2 (or page 1 if you are using a short form) must be in the correct location to be seen through the window envelope used to mail the certificate. For the address box to be properly located, the top line of the address box must be about 2 inches from the bottom edge of the form.

The Copyright Office is dedicated to issuing certificates of registration that provide an unmistakable and readable record of registered claims. You can help by making sure the information in your application is complete, accurate, and legible, and that the form itself is of an acceptable quality.

You can use fill-in forms on the Internet.

An applicant for copyright registration may select the proper form online at the Copyright Office Web site and type information directly onto the form instead of having to print the form and fill it in by hand or on a typewriter. After the form is filled in, it should be printed, signed, and mailed to the Copyright Office together with the deposit and the filing fee. At this time the Copyright Office does not accept electronic filings.

Who may use the fill-in forms?

Any applicant who has access to a computer with an Internet connection may fill in the form on the computer screen. Forms may be printed with either a laser or inkjet printer. Inkjet printer copies of the forms require enlarging if you use the "Shrink to Fit Page" option.

Which forms are available in fill-in version?

The forms currently existing in fill-in version are Forms PA, SE, SE/Group, SR, TX, VA, CA, CON, GATT, GATT/ GRP, GATT/ CON, and Short Forms PA, SE, TX, and VA. In the near future, the office expects to have fill-in versions for all forms. There is also a fill-in version of the Document Cover Sheet.

Where are the fill-in forms?

The fill-in forms are on the Copyright Office Web site at: **www. copyright.gov/forms**.

For Further Information

Information via the Internet: Frequently requested circulars, announcements, regulations, other related materials, and all copyright application forms are available via the Internet. You may access these from the Copyright Office Web site at **www. copyright.gov**.

Information by telephone: For general information about copyright, call the Copyright Public Information Office at (202) 707-3000. The TTY number is (202) 707-6737. Information specialists are on duty from 8:30 a.m. to 5:00 p.m., Eastern Time, Monday through Friday, except federal holidays. Recorded information is available 24 hours a day. Or, if you know which application forms and circulars you want, request them 24 hours a day from the Forms and Publications Hotline at (202)707-9100. Leave a recorded message.

Information by regular mail:

Write to:

Library of Congress
Copyright Office
Publications Section, LM-455
101 Independence Avenue, S.E.
Washington, D.C. 20559-6000

George Beauchamp received the first patent for the original "frying pan" electric guitar in 1931.

Chapter 4

Breakdown of Copyright Acts

"Intellectual property is an important legal and cultural issue. Society as a whole has complex issues to face here: private ownership vs. open source, and so on."

Tim Berners-Lee, English inventor

Copyright is the right granted by the laws of the United States to an author or other creator to control use of the work created. The copyright law grants owners of copyright (authors and other creators and publishers) the sole right to do or allow others to do each of the following acts with regard to their copyrighted works: reproduce all or part of the work, distribute copies, prepare new (derivative) versions based on the original work, or perform and display the work publicly.

Copyright protection covers both published and unpublished works. An out-of-print, previously published work does not lose its copyright.

Copyright protection exists to foster and induce the creation of all forms of works of authorship. The copyright holder has extensive rights. The copyright law provides fair returns to creators and copyright owners. To the extent that copies are made without permission, authors and publishers including faculty are deprived of revenues in the market for which they have written and published.

Copyright acts provide copyright protection beginning at the moment the work is created. Registration with the United States Copyright Office is not required in order for a work to be protected under United States copyright law. However, the copyright must generally be registered with the Copyright Office in Washington, D.C. before the copyright owner can sue an infringer.

In obtaining a copyright, the holder gains several exclusive rights typically attached to the holder of a copyright:

1. To produce copies or reproductions of the work and to sell those copies

2. To import or export the work

3. To create derivative works that adapt the original

4. To perform or display the work publicly

5. To sell or assign these rights to others

6. To transmit or display by radio or video

How the Acts Gave Affected the Laws Today

Given the three-year statute of limitations bar, there are only two relevant omnibus Copyright Acts relevant in litigation: the 1909 Act, as amended, and the 1976 Act, as amended. The easiest approach to the question of which act to apply would be to simply apply the 1909 Act to all questions about works created between March 1909 and December 31, 1977, when that act was in effect, and for the 1976 Act to apply to all works created on or after January 1, 1978. However even this simple approach has problems: What about works created before January 1, 1978, but not published or registered? Those works were previously protected under state law.

Act of 1790

The Copyright Act of 1790 was deliberated on and passed during the Second Session of Congress, convened on January 4, 1790. However, President George Washington did not sign the bill into law until May 31, 1790. Though most of the states had passed various legislation that secured copyrights following the Revolutionary War, the object of this act was the "encouragement of learning." The law covered only books, maps, and charts. Paintings, drawings, and music were not included until a later time. The act secured authors the "sole right and liberty of printing, reprinting, publishing, and vending" the copies of their books, charts, and maps. The term set on this act was 14 years, with the right to renew an additional 14-year term should the copyright holder still be alive.

The act borrowed from the 1709 Statute of Anne, as the first sentences of the two laws were nearly identical. Both required registration in order for a work to be deposited in officially designated repositories, such as the Library of Congress in the United States and Oxford and Cambridge Universities in the United Kingdom. The Copyright Act of 1790 was exclusive to United States citizens. Non-citizens of the United States could not be granted any copyright protection until the creation of the International Copyright Act of 1891.

Points garnered from the Copyright Act of 1790, the first copyright law in the United States, are:

- This law plainly grants copyright protection for books in their entirety, not for every last sentence in a book.

- Thus the insertion of certain wording, or the publishing of adaptations, translations, or other derivative works by others, was not overtly prohibited.

- Pictures, painting, or drawings, at this point have no copyright protection.

- This law explicitly excludes from protection books written or printed or published outside the U.S. by non-U.S. citizens.

- Copyright protection was for a term of 14 years, and could be extended for an additional 14 years if the author was still living at the end of the initial term.

- If a specific procedure was not followed, there was no copyright protection.

- The statute of limitations for copyright violation lasted for one year only.

This copyright law positioned numerous books in the public domain. The public domain is an enormous mass of intellectual property, which includes songs, books, movies, legislation, etc., that is open and available for the public to use freely. Works that are copyrighted fall into the public domain after a certain period of time, which has fluctuated a great deal over the past half century. In fact, copyright extensions have been increased at least 11 times over the past 40 years.

These books were thus believed to be fair game for use by future authors. Everyone and anyone could even legally reprint these books in their entirety. Anything published before 1923 is in the public domain. Before the Copyright Act of 1976, individuals were forced to register their created works with the Copyright Office in order to protect their works. If the creators failed to do so, they had little protection because there was no copyright of their work and it would then fall directly into the public domain. The first copyright entry for this act was *The Philadelphia Spelling Book* by John Barry, registered in the U.S. District Court of Pennsylvania on June 9, 1790.

However, in 1976, the Copyright Act was passed and gave automatic copyright protection to works once they were created. Unfortunately, there has not been a cumulative list of public domain works created for easy reference. This would be a daunting task because the list and rules are ever changing.

At present, the New America Foundation, also known as The Center for the Public Domain, is working toward protecting the present and future of the public domain through education and leadership. This organization has allocated different digital information that is likely to be in the public domain such as databases, open-source software, freeware, etc. Creative Commons is also a public domain-welcoming organization created by Lawrence Lessig, professor and attorney at Stanford University, that helps creators of works donate them to the public domain or creates licenses for the works for minimal fees.

Act of 1909

The Copyright Act of 1909 allowed for works to be copyrighted for a period of 28 years from the date of publication. This was a landmark statue in United States statutory copyright law. It was renewable once for a second 28-year period. Like the Act of 1790 before it, the copyrighted work could be extended for a second term of equal value, for a total of 28 years. This act gave federal statutory copyright protection to original works only when those works were either published or had a notice of copyright affixed to them. It was left up to individual state laws to protect unpublished works. For published works, whether they contained a notice of copyright or not, these are protected by federal law exclusively. Works without a notice of copyright affixed to them were then "published" in a legal sense only; the 1909 Act provided no copyright protection, and the work became part of the public domain. The original Copyright Act of 1909 balanced the individual's property rights with the public's need for creativity in the arts and sciences. Usage fees were charged and distributed to creators and publishers. New technology has made this system inadequate.

Act of 1976

The primary basis of copyright law is the Copyright Act of 1976. This Act spells out the basic rights of copyright holders and codified the doctrine of fair use, adopting for most new copyrights a unitary term based on the date of the author's death and not on a scheme of fixed initial and renewal terms. It was the first major revision to statutory copyright law in the United States since the 1909 Act. **Researchcopyright.com** notes that the Copyright Law Act of 1976 pre-empted all previous laws that were on the books in the United States, including the Copyright Act of 1909. Congress stated a revision was required because of extensive technological advances since the 1909 Act.

This act included television, sound recordings, motion pictures, and radio and was designed to, in part, address the intellectual property issues raised with these advanced forms of communication. The noteworthy portions of the act, through its terms, pre-empts all earlier copyright law in the United States. The pre-empted law includes previously mentioned federal legislation, such as the Copyright Act of 1909, but also includes all pertinent common law and state copyright laws as they clash with the act.

The Copyright Act of 1976 endorses a number of exclusive rights to copyright owners, including the:

- Reproduction right — the right to make copies of a protected work

- Distribution right — the right to sell or otherwise distribute copies to the public

- Right to create adaptations — the right to prepare new works based on the protected work (called derivative works)

- Performance and display rights — the right to perform a protected work or to display a work in public.

Berne Convention Implementation Act of 1988

Under the Berne Convention of 1886, copyrights for creative works do not have to be asserted or declared, as they are automatically in force at creation. An author need not register or apply for a copyright in countries that adhere to the convention laws. This is when the convention first established recognition of copyrights among sovereign nations, rather than merely bilaterally. The United States did not sign the Berne Convention until 1989.

At the instigation of Victor Hugo, the Berne Convention Implementation Act was originally the Association Litteraire et Artistique Internationale, which was influenced by the French right of the author. This was in direct contrast with the Anglo-Saxon concept of copyright, which concerned itself with economic issues.

The Berne Convention requires its signatories to recognize the copyright of works of authors from other signatory countries, known as members of the Berne Union, in the same way it recognizes the copyright of its own nationals — which means that, for instance, French copyright law applies to anything published or performed in France, regardless of where it was originally created.

The Convention rests on three basic principles of copyright law and contains a series of provisions determining the minimum protection to be granted to intellectual properties, as well as special provisions available to developing countries, usually members of the WIPO, which want to make use of them.

(1) The three basic principles are the following:

(a) Works originating in one of the contracting states (that is, works by an author who is a national of such a state, or works that were first published in such a state) must be given the same protection in each of the other contracting states as the latter grants to the works of its own nationals (principle of "national treatment").

(b) Such protection must not be conditional upon compliance with any formality (principle of "automatic" protection).

(c) Such protection is independent of the existence of protection in the country of origin of the work (principle of the "independence" of protection). If, however, a contracting state provides for a longer term than the minimum prescribed by the convention, and the work ceases to be protected in the country of origin, protection may be denied once protection in the country of origin ceases.

(2) The minimum standards of protection relate to the works and rights to be protected, and the duration of the protection:

(a) As to works, the protection must include "every production in the literary, scientific and artistic domain, whatever may be the mode or form of its expression" (Article 2(1) of the Convention).

(b) Subject to certain permitted reservations, limitations or exceptions.

(c) As to the duration of protection, the general rule is protection must be granted until the expiration of the 50th year after the author's death. There are, however, exceptions to this general rule. In the case of anonymous or pseudonymous works, the term of protection expires 50 years after the work has been lawfully made available to the public, except if the pseudonym leaves no doubt as to the author's identity or if the author discloses his identity during that period; in the latter case, the general rule applies. In the case of audiovisual (cinematographic) works, the minimum term of protection is 50 years after the making available of the work to the public or, failing such an event, from the creation of the work. In the case of works of applied art and photographic works, the minimum term is 25 years from the work's creation.

(3 Countries regarded as developing countries in conformity with the established practice of the General Assembly of the United Nations may, for certain works and under certain conditions, depart from these minimum standards of protection with regard to the right of translation and the right of reproduction.

The Berne Convention for the Protection of Literary and Artistic Works states that works are protected without any formality in all the countries party to that Convention. This means that international copyright protection is automatic; it exists as soon as a work is created, and this principle applies in all the countries party to the Berne Convention.

Sonny Bono Copyright Term Extension Act of 1998

The Copyright Term Extension Act (CTEA) or, as it is alternatively known, the Sonny Bono Copyright Term Extension, extended copyright terms in the United States by 20 years. Before this, the extension copyright lasted for the life of the author plus 50 years, or 75 years for the work of corporate authorship. This act extended these terms to the life of the author plus an additional 70 years. For work of corporate authorship, ownership was extended to 120 years after creation or 95 years after publication, whichever came first.

The CTEA was the project of former entertainer Sonny Bono, who later became an elected member of the House of Representatives. His life was cut short by a skiing accident in January 1998. His wife, Mary Bono, was elected to take his place in the House, and further sponsored the CTEA. "Actually, Sonny wanted the term of copyright protection to last forever. I am informed by staff that such a change would violate the constitution," Mary Bono said, speaking on the floor of the U.S. House of Representatives.

The goal of the CTEA was to increase the terms of copyright on literary, television and film works, and on characters from literature, television, and film. Under the CTEA, works at present under copyright were granted an additional 20 years of copyright status. The Supreme Court upheld the constitutionality of the CTEA. Proponents also indicate that the extension did not stop all works from going into the public domain. They also note that the 1976 Copyright Act establishment, in which unpublished works created before 1978 will enter the public domain by 2003, remained unchanged by the 1998 extension.

Therefore, a copyrighted work is protected for the life of the author, and then for 70 years after his or her death. For a copyrighted work or character that has been created through collaboration, copyright extends for the life of the authors and 95 years after their death.

Material created outside the U.S. that is established on a copyrighted character or theme cannot be sold within the U.S. For example, a video game featuring a copyrighted character that is created in Japan could not be sold legally in the U.S. The CTEA did not reinstate copyright status to those works, which had already passed into the public domain. It only applied to works that still maintain copyright status.

The CTEA has sometimes been referred to as the Mickey Mouse Act, since one of the main protections provided was for Disney characters like Mickey Mouse, which would soon lose their copyright status. In 1998, representatives of the Walt Disney Company came to Washington looking for help. Disney's copyright on Mickey Mouse, who made his screen debut in the

1928 cartoon short "Steamboat Willie," was due to expire in 2003, and Disney's rights to Pluto, Goofy, and Donald Duck were to expire a few years later. Rather than let Mickey and friends enter the public domain, Disney and its non-animated friends (a group of Hollywood studios, music labels, and content owners) told Congress they wanted an extension bill passed.

No Electronic Theft Act of 1997 (NET)

The No Electronic Theft Act of 1997 was originally supported by the software and entertainment industries and opposed by scientists, librarians, and academics. It stemmed from the concerns surrounding the protection of the copyrights of electronic data extending to computer software. Aimed primarily at the rampant theft of computer software, it allows the prosecution of anyone who violates the copyright of materials worth more than $1,000 in a six-month period by copying, distributing, or receiving software. Congress passed the law in November 1997 after the software and entertainment industries strongly lobbied for it, claiming losses amounting to $2 billion in 1996 in the United States alone. In particular, the law closed a narrow loophole in existing federal law, which made criminal prosecution for copyright violation only possible if the violation resulted in financial gain. NET was viewed as "closing a loophole" in the criminal law. Under the old statutory scheme, people who intentionally distributed copied software over the Internet did not face criminal penalties if they did not profit from their actions. The act was strongly backed by the software and entertainment industries but opposed by science and academic groups. The NET Act is applicable in situations such as running a file sharing application with outgoing transfers enabled, hosting files on a Web account, transferring files through Internet Relay Chat (IRC), and other methods of making copyrighted material available over networks.

According to the software industry, the decision paved the way for piracy of material through Web pages and other commonly used Internet sites. Software manufacturers were concerned about deliberate piracy by computer hackers and wanted to stop the casual lending and copying of computer software between consumers and within offices. Lobbyists pointed to what became known as the "LaMaccia loophole." This term refers to an unforeseen weakness in federal law that was exposed by the failed federal prosecution of computer hacker David LaMacchia in 1994. The NET Act was designed to close the LaMacchia loophole. Swiftly passed by the House and subsequently approved by the Senate, the act accomplished this by amending two key parts of federal copyright law. The law previously defined copyright violation strictly in terms of financial gain. The NET Act broadened them to include the reproduction or distribution of one or more copies of copyrighted works and considers financial gain simply to be the possession of copyrighted work. It defines a misdemeanor violation as occurring when the value of the copied material exceeds $1,000 over a 180-day period; a felony occurs if the value exceeds $2,500. Penalties range from a one-year jail sentence and up to $100,000 in fines for first-time offenders, to five years' imprisonment, and up to $250,000 in fines for repeat offenders.

The NET Act's highlights are:

- Makes it a crime to circumvent anti-piracy measures built into most commercial software.

- Outlaws the manufacture, sale, or distribution of code-cracking devices used to illegally copy software.

- Permits the cracking of copyright protection devices to conduct encryption research, assess product interoperability, and test computer security systems.

- Provides exemptions from anti-circumvention provisions for nonprofit libraries, archives, and educational institutions under certain circumstances.

- In general, limits Internet service providers from copyright infringement liability for simply transmitting information over the Internet.

- Service providers, however, are expected to remove material from users' Web sites that appears to constitute copyright infringement.

- Limits liability of nonprofit institutions of higher education (when they serve as online service providers and under certain circumstances) for copyright infringement by faculty members or graduate students.

- Requires that "Webcasters" pay licensing fees to record companies.

- Requires that the Register of Copyrights, after consultation with relevant parties, submit to Congress' recommendations regarding how to promote distance education through digital technologies while "maintaining an appropriate balance between the rights of copyright owners and the needs of users."

- States explicitly that nothing in this section shall affect rights, remedies, limitations, or defenses to copyright infringement, including fair use.

Digital Millennium Act of 1998

The Digital Millennium Copyright Act (DMCA) criminalizes production and dissemination of technology, devices, or services used to circumvent measures, which control access to copyrighted works. The law criminalizes the act of avoiding an access control, even when there is no breach of copyright itself. It also intensifies the penalties for copyright infringement on the World Wide Web or Internet. President Bill Clinton signed the Act into law. The DMCA amended Title 17 of the United States Code to extend the reach of copyright, while restricting the legal responsibility of online providers from copyright infringement by their users. This act implements two World Intellectual Property Organization (WIPO) treaties. Technically, the DMCA even prohibits consumers from altering the playback of a DVD in any way. This casts a shadow on DVD technology available from companies like ClearPlay, which removes potentially offensive violence, sexuality, and language from DVD movies.

Family Entertainment and Copyright Act of 2005

The basics of the Family Entertainment and Copyright Act of 2005 state that any person who, without the authorization of the copyright owner, knowingly uses or attempts to use an audiovisual recording device to transmit or make a copy of a motion picture or other audiovisual work that is protected under the laws of copyright can be punished with imprisonment for not more than 3 years, a fine, or both; or, if the offense is a second or subsequent offense, imprisonment for no more than 6 years, a fine, or both.

Any person who deliberately infringes upon a copyright shall be punished as granted under current laws of protection. Criminal infringement shall be determined by the following criteria: if the infringement was committed for purposes of commercial advantage or private financial gain, by the reproduction or distribution, including by electronic means, during any 180-day period, of one or more copies or phono-records of one or more copyrighted works, which have a total retail value of more than $1,000; or by the distribution of a work being prepared for commercial distribution, by making it available on a computer network accessible to members of the public, if such person knew or should have known that the work was intended for commercial distribution.

Performance Rights Act of 2007

The Performance Rights Act of 2007 is a bill to provide fair compensation to artists for use of their sound recordings. It is not yet a law, but on December 18, 2007 it was referred to the Senate committee. The current status is that it has been read twice, referred to the Committee on the Judiciary, and is still awaiting a vote.

The Classroom Exemption Act

Section 110 under the Copyright Act, sometimes called the classroom exemption, is a public performance and/or public show restriction, which provide exemptions on the exclusive rights of copyright holders. These exemptions allow educators and students to perform and display copyrighted works within the classroom. Note that this exemption applies to classrooms only, not the Internet. Face-to-face instruction is the only place where non-profit educational institutions can show movies or other audio-visual digital works.

Amend Chapter 1 of Title 17

This amendment declares that it is not a copyright infringement for churches and qualified church-controlled organizations to communicate a transmission of a professional football contest so long as no direct charge is made to see or hear the transmission, no money is accepted or received by the organization during the communication, and the transmission is not further retransmitted.

This is a bill designed to amend Chapter 1 of Title 17, United States Code, to provide an exemption from exclusive rights in copyright for certain nonprofit organizations to display live football games, and for other purposes. It has not yet been passed, but as of February 4, 2008 it was referred to the Senate committee. The current status is that it has been read twice and referred to the Committee on the Judiciary.

Intellectual Property Enforcement Act of 2007

This act makes copyright registration requirements applicable to only civil but not criminal copyright infringement actions. It authorizes the court to make rulings in civil copyright infringement actions.

The Intellectual Property Enforcement Act of 2007 is a bill to amend Titles 17 and 18, United States Code, and the Trademark Act of 1946 to strengthen and harmonize the protection of intellectual property, and for other purposes. It amends the Treasury and General Government Appropriations Act of 2000 to repeal provisions establishing the National Intellectual Property

Law Enforcement Coordination Council. It also establishes the Intellectual Property Enforcement Network (IPEN), consisting of specified representatives of various government agencies, to: (1) establish policies, objectives, and priorities concerning international intellectual property protection and law enforcement; (2) coordinate and facilitate implementation of such policies, objectives, and priorities; and (3) protect U.S. intellectual property rights overseas, including by creating an international task force.

Shawn Bentley Orphan Works Act of 2008

The Shawn Bentley Orphan Works Act of 2008 is a bill to provide a limitation on judicial remedies in copyright infringement cases involving orphan works. It has not yet passed, but on May 15, 2008, it was placed on the Senate Legislative Calendar under General Orders. The history of this act began in 2005, when the United States Copyright Office studied issues raised by "orphan works" (copyrighted works whose owners may be impossible to identify and locate). Concerns had been raised that the uncertainty surrounding ownership of such works might needlessly discourage subsequent creators and users from incorporating such works in new creative efforts, or from making such works available to the public.

The office issued a Federal Register Notice summarizing issues raised by orphan works, and soliciting written comments from all interested parties. The office asked specifically whether there were compelling concerns raised by orphan works that merit a legislative, regulatory, or other solution, and if so, what type of solution could effectively address these concerns without conflicting with the legitimate interests of authors and right holders.

International Filing Systems

There is no single way to obtain international protection of intellectual property. The closest current approaches to such international protection are those provided by the following conventions establishing international application filing systems.

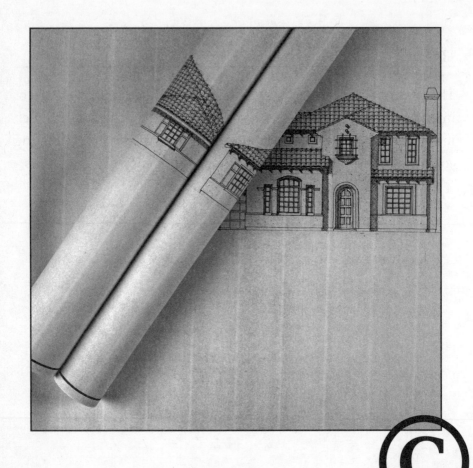

Copyright law started including architectual drawings on Dec. 1, 1990. The law only applies to plans and drawings created on or after the effective date.

Chapter 5

Copyright Ownership & Rights

"The primary objective of copyright is not to reward the labor of authors, but 'to promote the Progress of Science and useful Arts.' To this end, copyright assures authors the right to their original expression, but encourages others to build freely upon the ideas and information conveyed by a work. This result is neither unfair nor unfortunate. It is the means by which copyright advances the progress of science and art."

Justice Sandra Day O'Connor, Feist Publications, Inc. v. Rural Telephone Service Co., 1991

Copyright ownership and its rights can be confusing, especially since copyright applies to a broader group of works than ever before. In addition to photographs, advertising, and motion pictures, copyright's scope has been made more comprehensive by courts and Congress to include the generally defined areas of literary works, musical works (including any supplementary words, dramatic works, including any associated music, pantomimes, and choreographic work), pictorial, graphic, and sculptural works, motion pictures and other audiovisual works, sound recordings, and architectural works — so broadly interpreted that computer code and databases count as literary works and something as indistinct as "look and feel" meets the criteria as audiovisual.

The author of a work is the initial owner of the copyright in it and may exploit the work him or herself, or transfer some or all the rights conferred by the copyright to others.

Who is an Author?

According to the U.S. Copyright Office, an author is defined by copyright law as the creator or author of the original expression in a work. The author is also the owner of copyright unless there is a written agreement by which the author assigns the copyright to another person or entity, such as a publisher.

Works Made-For-Hire

A work made-for-hire is when the writer agrees to perform or produce any number of concise, objective, and original works for a publisher. The length of said work should be determined before accepting any such agreement. The publisher usually reserves the right to reject any of the writer's work that does not meet their standards. Final judgment is generally the sole responsibility of the publisher and/or the client. In most made-for-hire agreements, not only is the length agreed upon before the work starts, but a deadline also is set. In these cases the writer is considered an independent contractor, not the client's employee. Be sure to read the contract before agreeing to any such deal to ensure you know exactly what is expected from you and what the publisher or client expects. The writer and client agree generally to the following: the writer may work for other clients at the same time, yet not disclose the project from the first client; the writer has the sole right to control and direct the means, manner and method by which the services required by the agreement will be performed; the writer has the right to perform the services by the agreement at any place, location or time; and the client or publisher agrees not to withhold Social Security and Medicare taxes from the writer's payment or make FICA payments on the writer's behalf. And finally, the writer is ineligible to participate in any employee pension, health, vacation pay, sick pay, or other fringe benefit plan of the publisher or client.

Copyright law gives copyright holders exclusive control over their works. Usually, if someone wants to use all or even a portion of the copyrighted material, then permission is needed. United States Copyright law refers to "works-for-hire" or labor executed in the normal course of employment. Generally, the work completed in this context belongs to the employer. Intellectual property ownership includes any work of authorship entitled to protection under the copyright laws. The writer's work, in order to be deemed a made-for-hire project, must have been specially ordered and commissioned by the publisher or client as a contribution to a collective work eligible to be treated as a work made-for-hire under the United States Copyright Act. The publisher shall be the sole author of the writer's work and any work embodying the writer's work, according to the United States Copyright Act. In the end, the writer agrees not to use any of the intellectual property mentioned in the agreement or contract with the client or publisher for the benefit for any other party without the publisher's or client's prior written consent.

However, over the years, much of the work that academics have created, like research texts and other publications, has been copyrighted to that person, even if these works were created during the regular course of employment.

At most educational institutions, the copyright holders of online courses and materials fall into one of three categories:

1. The policy explicitly gives ownership of publications to the faculty.

2. The institution explicitly claims copyright.

3. No policy exists.

Collaborations

How is copyright distributed when there are two or more writers or collaborators on a project?

Copyright in each separate contribution to a collective work is distinct from copyright in the collective work as a whole, and rests initially in the author of the contribution. In the absence of an express transfer of the copyright or of any rights under it, the owner of copyright in the collective work is presumed to have acquired only the privilege of reproducing and distributing the contribution as part of that particular collective work, any revision of that collective work, and any later collective work in the same series.

Transfer of Copyright

Are copyrights transferable?

Yes. Like any other property, the owner may transfer all or part of the rights in a work to another. The ownership of a copyright may be transferred in whole or in part by any means of conveyance or by operation of law, and may be bequeathed by will or pass as personal property by the applicable laws of intestate succession.

An involuntary transfer is when an individual author's ownership of a copyright, or of any of the exclusive rights under a copyright, has not previously been transferred voluntarily by that individual author, and no action has been taken by any governmental body or other official or organization purporting to seize, expropriate, transfer, or exercise rights of ownership with respect to the copyright.

Do you have any forms for transfer of copyrights?

There are no forms provided by the United States Copyright Office to affect a copyright transfer. The Office does, however, keep records of transfers if they are submitted. Transfers of copyright are normally made by contract. The Copyright Office does not have any forms for such transfers. The law does provide for the recording in the Copyright Office of transfers of copyright ownership. Copyright is a personal property right, and it is subject to the various state laws and regulations that govern the ownership, inheritance, or transfer of personal property as well as terms of contracts or conduct of business.

TRANSFER OF COPYRIGHT OWNERSHIP (EXAMPLE FORM)

For one dollar ($1.00) and other important consideration, the receipt of which is acknowledged, the undersigned transfers to _____ all rights included in a copyright in the work(s) described below, including, but not restricted to, the exclusive right to do and to authorize any one or all of the following:

(a) To reproduce the work

(b) To prepare derivative works

(c) To distribute copies of the work to the public by sale or other transfer of ownership, or by rental, lease, or lending

(d) To publicly perform and display the work

TRANSFER OF COPYRIGHT OWNERSHIP (EXAMPLE FORM)

This transfer includes the original

- Literary

- Pictorial, graphic and sculptural

- Audiovisual

- Sound recording

- Work(s) of authorship by the undersigned described below, and/or copies of which are attached

Describe the contact of the photo(s).

This document also transfers and conveys ownership of all material objects in or on which the described work(s) is embodied.

It is warranted that ownership of the described work(s) and material object(s) is in the undersigned, and there are no prior transfers or licenses or rights in the described work(s).

Signed this day of _____ , 20__.

Owner/Author

Name

Address

STATE OF

COUNTY OF

This Transfer of Copyright Ownership was duly acknowledged before me, a Notary Public, on the day of _____ , 20__, by (Owner/Author).

Notary Public

County

My Commission expires:

Exclusive Rights

What are the logistics of exclusive rights, and where is the public domain?

The United States Copyright Office defines the public domain not as a place, but that a work of authorship is in the public domain if it is no longer under copyright protection or if it failed to meet the requirements for copyright protection. Works in the public domain may be used freely without the permission of the former copyright owner.

What is an ISBN number?

The International Standard Book Number, ISBN, is controlled by the R.R. Bowker Company, 877-310-7333. The ISBN is a numerical identifier to aid the international community in recognizing and ordering specific publications.

Investigating the Status of a Copyrighted Work

According to the United States Copyright Office, there are several ways to investigate whether a work is under copyright protection and, if so, the facts of the copyright. There are three main ones. Examine a copy of the work for such elements as a copyright notice, place and date of publication, author, and publisher. If the work is a sound recording, examine the disc, tape cartridge, or cassette in which the recorded sound is fixed, or the album cover, sleeve, or container in which the recording is sold. Make a search of the United States Copyright Office catalogs and other records, or you can have the United States Copyright Office make a search for you.

Copyright investigations frequently entail more than one of these methods. Even if you pursue all three methods, the results may not be irrefutable. In addition, as described in this book and by the U.S. Copyright Office, the changes brought about under the Copyright Act of 1976, the Berne Convention Implementation Act of 1988, the Copyright Renewal Act of 1992, and the Sonny Bono Copyright Term Extension Act of 1998 must be measured when examining the copyright status of a work. It is vital to understand that this book holds only general information and that there are a number of omissions to the principles outlined here. In numerous cases it is significant to seek advice from a copyright attorney before making any conclusions regarding the copyright status of a work.

The United States Copyright Office offers this advice when searching copyright office records and catalogs: "The Copyright Office published the Catalog of Copyright Entries (CCE) in printed format from 1891 through 1978. From 1979 through 1982 the CCE was issued in microfiche format. The catalog was divided into parts according to the classes of works registered. Each CCE segment covered all registrations made during a particular period of time. Renewal registrations made from 1979 through 1982 are found in Section 8 of the catalog. Renewals prior to that time were generally listed at the end of the volume containing the class of work to which they pertained. A number of libraries throughout the U.S. maintain copies of the Catalog, and this may provide a good starting point if you wish to make a search yourself. There are some cases, however, in which a search of the Catalog alone will not be sufficient to provide the needed information. For example: Because the Catalog does not include entries for assignments or other recorded documents, it cannot be used for searches involving the ownership of rights. The Catalog entry contains the essential facts concerning a registration, but it is not a verbatim transcript of the registration record. It does not contain the address of the copyright claimant. Effective with registrations made since 1982 when the CCE was discontinued, the only method of searching outside the Library of Congress is by using the Internet to access the automated catalog. The automated catalog contains entries from 1978 to the present."

American copyright is becoming more internationalized. The World Intellectual Property Organization (WIPO) has been the foremost player in this effort. Membership to the World Trade Organization (WTO) is predicated on agreement with the Trade Related aspects of Intellectual Property rights (TRIPS) agreement, which regulates, and in most cases extends, the reach of copyright. Proponents of the Sonny Bono CTEA claimed harmonization with European copyright as their highest goal, since copyright law in Europe has an uncommon history and form from United States and British copyright. For example, there is no idea of fair use, authors have so-called moral rights to their works, and the terms lasted considerably longer than United States copyright terms. In most cases, law has coordinated by giving the most control to copyright holders, leveling the field at the higher common denominator of jurisdiction.

Fair Use

What is fair use?

Fair use is a United States legal doctrine that permits certain usage of copyright material without requiring permission of the copyright owner. It has been invoked in a number of cases.

Fair use is founded on the belief that the public is at liberty to freely use pieces of copyrighted materials for purposes of commentary and criticism. The fair use privilege is perhaps the most important restriction on a copyright owner's exclusive rights. "Fair use doctrine provides a set of guidelines pursuant to which researchers, educators, scholars, and others may use copyrighted works without seeking permission or paying royalties. Fair use doctrine does not provide a right to use somebody else's work, but presents a defense against accusations of copyright violation for people who reasonably believed that their use of a copyrighted work was fair use. That means that if your use is challenged, you will have the burden of proving that your use qualified as 'fair use'" (Fair Use Doctrine and Copyright Law by Aaron Larson, Law Offices of Aaron Larson, September 2003).

How much of someone else's work can you use without getting permission?

The fair use doctrine of the United States copyright statute states that it is permissible to use incomplete segments of a work including quotes, for purposes such as commentary, criticism, news reporting, and scholarly reports.

Fair use guidelines for multimedia

Text

- Up to 10 percent of a copyrighted work or 1,000 words, whichever is less

Poems

- Entire poem if less than 250 words

- 250 or less if longer poem

- No more than five poems (or excerpts) of different poets, from an anthology

- Only three poems (or excerpts) per poet

Motion Media

- Up to 10 percent of a copyrighted work or three minutes, whichever is less

- Clip cannot be altered in any way

Music

- Up to 10 percent of a copyrighted musical composition, but no more than half a minute

- Up to 10 percent of a body of sound recording, but no more than half a minute

- Any alterations cannot change the basic melody or the fundamental character of the work

Internet

- Internet resources will often combine both copyrighted and public domain sites; therefore care should be used in downloading any sites for use in multimedia presentations.

- Until further clarification, educators and students are advised to write to the copyright holder for permission to use Internet resources and to be mindful of the copyright ramifications of including embedded additional links to that particular site.

Copying and Distribution Limitations

- Do not post multimedia projects claiming fair use exemption on an unsecured Web site.

- No more than two copies of the original production may be made.

- Only one may be placed on reserve for others to use for instructional purposes.

- An additional copy may be made for preservation purposes, but may be used or copied only to replace a use copy that has been lost, damaged, or stolen.

- If more than one person has created the multimedia presentation, each principal creator may retain only one copy.

Permission Requirements

- For multimedia projects used for non-educational or commercial purposes

- For duplication or distribution of multimedia projects beyond limitations outlined above

Could you be sued for using somebody else's work?
What about quotes or samples?

When using a copyrighted work devoid of authorization, the owner may be at liberty to bring an infringement action against you. There are situations under the fair use doctrine where a quote or a sample may be used with no permission.

Do you need to obtain permission for images on the Library of Congress Web site that you would like to use?

With few exceptions, the Library of Congress does not own copyright to the materials in its collections and does not grant or deny permission to use the content mounted on its Web site.

Copyright in an Electronic World

Students may use portions of lawfully obtained copyrighted works in their academic multimedia projects, with proper credit and citations. They may retain them in personal portfolios as examples of their academic work. Students and teachers must incorporate on the opening screen of their programs and on any printed materials that their presentation has been prepared under fair use exemption of the United States Copyright Law and is restricted from further use. Educators may claim fair use for their own productions providing these productions are:

- For face-to-face curriculum-based instruction

- Demonstrations of how to create multimedia productions

- Presented at conferences (but you may not share copies of the actual production)

- For remote instruction as long as the distribution signal is limited

- Kept for only two years

Fair use ends when the multimedia originator loses control of his product's use, such as when others access it over the Internet. Educators or students need not write for permission if their presentation falls within the specific multimedia fair use guidelines; educators and students are advised to note that if there is a possibility that their own educational multimedia project incorporating copyrighted works under fair use could later result in broader distribution, whether or not as a commercial product, it is strongly recommended they take steps to obtain permission during the development process for all copyrighted portions rather than waiting until after completion of the project.

Chapter 6

Excluded Material for Copyright

"Earlier generations of technology ... have presented challenges to existing copyright law, but none have posed the same threat as the digital age."

John V. Pavlik, New Media Technology, 1996

Copyright laws do not protect everything. In order to ensure the protection of your intellectual property, certain criteria have been established to recognize it as being able to be protected. This chapter focuses on what materials are not eligible for protection.

What Type of Material is Excluded for Copyright?

A number of categories of material are ineligible for federal copyright protection. These include, among others:

a. Works that have not been fixed in a tangible form of expression (i.e. choreographic works that have not been notated or recorded, or improvisational speeches or performances that have not been written or recorded)

b. Titles, names, short phrases, and slogans; recognizable symbols or designs; simple variations of typographic ornamentation, lettering, or coloring; lists of ingredients or contents

C. Ideas, procedures, methods, systems, processes, concepts, principles, discoveries, or devices, as distinguished from a description, explanation, or illustration

Works consisting completely of information that is common property and containing no original authorship, i.e., standard calendars, height and weight charts, tape measures and rulers, and lists or tables taken from public documents or other common sources.

What can and cannot be copied in the public domain?

Works of the United States Government are considered public domain, so copyright laws are not enforced or pursued.

Publications incorporating U. S. Government Works

Works by the U. S. government are not eligible for U. S. copyright protection. For works published on and after March 1, 1989, the previous notice requirement for works consisting primarily of one or more U. S. government works has been removed. Use of a notice on such a work will beat a claim of innocent infringement, provided the notice also contains a statement that identifies either those sections of the work in which copyright is claimed or those portions that constitute U. S. government material.

> Example: © 2006 Jane Brown. Copyright claimed in Chapters 7-10, exclusive of U.S. government maps.

Copies of works published before March 1, 1989 that consists primarily of one or more works of the U. S. government should have a notice and the identifying statement.

Chapter 7

Copyright Duration & Process

"Copyright law is totally out of date. It is a Gutenberg artifact. Since it is a reactive process, it will probably have to break down completely before it is corrected."

Nicholas Negroponte, Being Digital, 1995

As with anything of worth, there are limits to the duration and protection of copyrighting. Carefully read the duration and process by which your intellectual property is going to be protected. A copyright registration is effective once the U.S. Copyright Office receives the copyright application and the work. There is a fallacy among many that copyright registration is only effective when issued a copyright certificate. However, that is not the case.

Once the copyright application and work arrive at the U.S. Copyright Office, the copyright registration is effective and your work is provided with full copyright protection.

How Long Does Copyright Protection Endure?

Works originally created on or after January 1, 1978

A work that was created or fixed in tangible form for the first time, on or after January 1, 1978, is automatically protected from the instant of its creation and is generally given a term lasting for the author's life plus an additional 70 years after the author's death. In the case of "a joint work prepared by two or more authors who did not work for hire," the term endures for 70 years after the last surviving author's death.

For works made for hire, and for anonymous and pseudonymous works, unless the author's identity is discovered in Copyright Office records, the length of copyright will be 95 years from publication or 120 years from creation, whichever is shorter.

Works originally created before January 1, 1978, but not published or registered by that date

These works have been automatically brought under the statute and are now given federal copyright protection. The duration of copyright in these works is generally computed in the same way as for works created on or after January 1, 1978: the life-plus-70 or 95/120-year terms apply to them as well. The law bestows that in no case would the term of copyright for works in this category expire before December 31, 2002, and for works published on or before December 31, 2002, the term of copyright will not expire before December 31, 2047.

Registration Procedures: Original Registration

To register a work, send the following three elements in the same envelope or package: a properly completed application form, a nonrefundable filing fee for each application, and a non-returnable deposit of the work being registered. The deposit requirements vary in particular situations. The general requirements should be sent to:

Library of Congress

Copyright Office

101 Independence Avenue, SE

Washington, D.C. 20559-6000

While you cannot copyright your Elvis sighting, you can copyright your photos. However, remember that someone else may have taken a similar photo and that copyright protects the individual photo, not the photo's subject matter

Chapter 8

Infringement of Copyright

"To promote public education and creative exchange, [copyright law] invites audiences and subsequent authors to use existing works in every conceivable manner that falls outside the province of the copyright owner's exclusive rights. Copyright law's perennial dilemma is to determine where exclusive rights should end and unrestrained public access should begin."

Neil Weinstock Netanel, "Copyright and a Democratic Civil Society," Yale Law Journal, 1996

People seek to protect their intellectual property because they do not wish for someone else to take their work and profit from it. That is called copyright infringement. This area of copyright law can be confusing and overwhelming, but this chapter is designed to answer the questions you may have in regards to copyright infringement.

What Infringes Copyright?

Using a substantial portion of work without giving recognition, or having the authorization or a license from the copyright owner or the owner's agent, is considered infringement. "A substantial portion" is a comparative term and depends on the character of the excerpt taken and its weight to the overall essence of the copyrighted material. The quality of the material taken is often more significant than the quantity. It is the quality or fundamental nature of what has been taken rather than the amount that is taken that will often determine whether the portion taken is "substantial."

Use of a substantial portion of copyright material is not an infringement if the use falls within one of the statutory fair dealing exceptions to copyright. These exceptions are for the purposes of: research or study, criticism or review, reporting the news, and judicial proceedings or professional legal advice.

The 10 percent rule

Material used for the intention of research or study is required to fall within the 10 percent rule. For the exception to apply, the material used must be less than 10 percent of the entire material, a single journal article, or one chapter of a book that is less than 10 pages.

Copyright v. plagiarism

Copyright infringement is different from plagiarism. Plagiarism is concerned with the unethical use of other people's ideas, whereas copyright relates to the legal implications of copying a work.

What does the future hold for copyright law?

Copyright law in the United States seems to have been written by lobbyists for publishers and motion picture studios, considering that legal protection for rights of authors is markedly less than in France or Germany, or even in the Berne Convention. However, as evidenced by the recent writer's strike in Hollywood, more and more protection is in store for authors.

What can I do if somebody infringed my copyright?

A group may request to protect his or her copyrights against illegal use by filing a civil lawsuit in federal district court. If you consider that your copyright has been infringed, discuss it with an attorney. In cases of willful infringement for profit, the United States Attorney may begin a criminal investigation.

How much do I have to change in order to claim copyright in someone else's work?

Merely the owner of copyright in a work has the privilege to put in order, or to authorize someone else to create, an original version of that work. For that reason, you cannot claim copyright to another's work, no matter how much you alter it, except if you have the owner's permission.

Copyright Terminology

All rights reserved

A phrase that was required as part of a copyright notice by the Buenos Aires Convention international treaty stating that all copyrighted works, barring those that are first published in a handful of North American and South American countries, is the assertion "All rights reserved." A copyright declaration is a pointless chaff. Moreover, for copyrighted works that are first published outside of North America and South America, the phrase has always been pointless chaff.

Anonymous

An author's contribution is anonymous when the author is not identified on the copies of the work.

Assignment of copyright

This means the transfer of all or partial portions of the copyright to a new owner.

Author

Author is the subject of copyright protection if one of three requirements are met: the person creates the work, the person or company pays another to create the work in employment context, or the person or company commissions the work under a valid work made-for-hire contract.

Author as owner of copyright

This occurs when an author assigns all of the copyright ownership rights to another party before the work is created, or when a work is created by an employee in the course of employment or as a commissioned work under a valid work made-for-hire contract.

Based on earlier work

Used to reference when an original piece of authorship has been based on an earlier version for its content and expression.

Certificate of registration

A certificate of registration is awarded when the United States Copyright Office approves a copyright application.

Characters, fictional

Fictional characters are protected separately from their original works as derivative copyrights, provided they are sufficiently unique and distinctive. A fictional character is any person, persona, identity, or entity whose existence originates from a fictional work or performance. Some fictional characters are based on adaptations of fact or non-fiction.

Co-authors

This is when two or more people contribute significant creative input to a work of expression.

Compulsory license

This refers to when permission must be obtained from the copyright owner for a work to be used.

Copyright

A form of protection provided by the laws of the United States for "original works of authorship" including literary, dramatic, musical, architectural, cartographic, choreographic, pantomimic, pictorial, graphic, sculptural, and audiovisual creations.

Copyright claimant

The party considered to be the basic owner of the copyright in a work registered with the United States Copyright Office.

Copyright Arbitration Royalty Panel (CARP)

When the affected parties cannot come to a voluntary agreement, a CARP is convened to determine royalty rate adjustments and the distribution of royalty funds collected by the Licensing Division. The CARP system consists of an ad hoc arbitration panel that recommended the royalty rates and distribution of royalty fees collected under certain of the statutory licenses and set some of the terms and conditions of some of the statutory licenses.

Copyright Office History Documents (COHD)

This program is an index to recorded documents from 1978 to the present that transfer copyright ownership or that pertains to a copyright.

Copyrighted work

A copyrighted work is awarded copyright protection.

Deposit (noun)

The copy, copies, or phono-records of an original work of authorship that are located in the Copyright Office to maintain the claim to copyright in the work or to meet the mandatory deposit conditions of the 1976 Copyright Act.

Deposit (verb)

To send to the Copyright Office a copy, copies, or phono-records of an original work of authorship to sustain a claim to copyright or to meet the mandatory deposit obligation of the 1976 Copyright Act.

Deposit account

Money kept in a special account set up in the Copyright Office by individuals or firms from which copyright fees are deducted.

Derivative work

A derivative work is one based on existing material to which enough original creative work that has been added so it now represents an original work of authorship. A typical example of a derivative work received for registration in the Copyright Office is one that is primarily a new work but incorporates some previously published material. This previously published material makes the work a derivative work under the copyright law. To be copyrightable, a derivative work must be different enough from the original to be regarded as a "new work" or must contain a substantial amount of new material. Making slight alterations or additions of little substance to a pre-existing work will not meet the criteria for the work to be seen as a new version for copyright purposes. The new material in it has to be original and copyrightable. Titles, short phrases, and format, for example, are not copyrightable.

Document

This refers to a paper relating to the ownership of a copyright or to any other material involving a copyright. Documents will be recorded in the Copyright Office for public record.

Ephemeral recording

Under some instances, the Copyright Act does allow the making of copies of works for purposes of later transmission. An ephemeral recording is a reproduction of a work produced exclusively for the purpose of a transmission of the work by an entity legally entitled to publicly perform the work.

Expedited registration

A special procedure to rapidly register a work if a copyright owner needs the registration to pursue a copyright infringement action in court.

Factual works, defined

Factual works are those that legitimately may be classified as nonfiction or historical.

Fair use

It is not an infringement of copyright to make short quotations from a work for purposes of criticism, comment, teaching, scholarship, or research.

Fixed in a tangible medium of expression

When an original work of authorship first qualifies for copyright protection when it is reduced to some physical form or representation.

Form of Notice for Visually Perceptible Copies

The notice for visually perceptible copies should contain all of the following three elements: the symbol © (the letter C in a circle) or the word "Copyright" or the abbreviation "Copr."; the author of the work; and the year of first publication of the work. Example: © 2006 John Doe.

Freedom of speech and copyright protection

The First Amendment of the U.S. Constitution states that the government is prohibited from placing restrictions on a person's freedom of speech, except in certain situations. Freedom of speech is the right to freely say what one pleases, as well as the related right to hear what others have stated. Recently, it has been commonly understood as encompassing full freedom of expression, including the freedom to create and distribute movies, pictures, songs, dances, and all other forms of expressive communication.

Grant of rights

When an author awards all copyright rights to his or her publisher in advance of publication in exchange for future royalties or other payment.

Identifying material, defined

In order to obtain a copyright, it is generally accepted that copies, or at least one, of complete volumes of the work are to be deposited with the United States Copyright Office.

Instructional text

A literary, pictorial, or graphic work prepared for use in daily instructional activities as an instructional text.

Internet Relay Chat (IRC)

Internet Relay Chat is a worldwide service you can use to send text messages to other people over the Internet.

Joint work

Under the Copyright Act of 1976, a joint work is considered "a work prepared by two or more authors who intend to merge their contributions into inseparable or interdependent parts of the original."

Licensing of copyrights

This is the method by which the owner of a copyright gives permission for another to use or copy an original work of authorship.

Parody and fair use

Parody happens when one work ridicules another well-known work by imitating it in a comedic way.

Peer-to-peer (P2P) networking

The type of network where computers converse immediately with each other, rather than through a central server and that frequently refers to merely as peer-to-peer, or abbreviated P2P, a type of network in which each workstation has equal capabilities and tasks. This differs from client/server architectures, in which some computers are devoted to serving other computers.

Photocopies and copyright law

With a few exceptions, making even one copy of an original work of authorship requires the copyright owner's permission; thus, copying without permission constitutes infringement.

Plagiarism

It is a violation of copyright law to use all or any part of A's document, either verbatim or with trivial changes, in a document written by B, except as described in the section on fair use.

Public domain

Any work of authorship that is not protected under copyright law is said to be in the public domain.

Publish

To publish a work is to allocate copies or phono-records of the work to the public by sale or other reassignment of ownership, or by rental, lease, or lending. Publication also includes submission to distribute copies or phono-records to a group of persons for purposes of further distribution, public performance, or public display.

Pseudonym domain: copyright context

Any work in which the author is identified by a fictitious name.

Registration of copyright

Copyright protection is automatically attached to any work of authorship when it is fixed in a tangible medium of expression.

Single registration rule

The USCO generally permits one registration for each original work of authorship.

Special relief

Special relief refers to when a special variance is granted to depart from its usual requirements for copyright registration.

Thin copyright

This occurs when a work features a limited number of original features, the copyright is thus referred to as being "thin."

Unpublished work, copyright ability of

An original work of authorship that is in a tangible medium

of expression but has not yet been published and then made available to the public without restriction, automatically qualifies for copyright protection.

Chapter 9

Trademarks at a Glance

"An image ... is not simply a trademark, a design, a slogan, or an easily remembered picture. It is a studiously crafted personality profile of an individual, institution, corporation, product, or service."

Daniel J. Boorstin, American social historian and educator

What is a Trademark?

A trademark is a word, graphic symbol, logo, phrase, or other device used to distinguish a specific manufacturer or seller's products and differentiate them from the products of another. Trademarks make it uncomplicated for consumers to swiftly identify the source of a particular good. A service mark is virtually the same as a trademark, the only dissimilarity being that trademarks are used to advocate products whereas service marks promote services. Also, in addition to a label, logo, or other associated symbol, a product may also come to be recognized by its unique shape. This is known as trade dress. By making goods simpler to identify, trademarks also provide manufacturers a motivation to invest in the superiority of their goods. Under some situations, trademark protection can reach beyond words, symbols, and phrases, or shapes to include other features of a product, like the color or its packaging.

What Sources of Law Oversee Trademarks?

Both state and federal law rule trademarks and initially, state common law granted the main source of protection for trademarks. However, in the late 1800s, the United States Congress passed the first federal trademark law. Federal trademark law has expanded repeatedly since then, taking over much of the ground originally covered by state common law. The main federal statute is the Lanham Act, which was enacted in 1946, and was most recently amended in 1996.

A mark should be distinctive, in order to function as a trademark. It must be capable of identifying the source of a specific good. In determining whether a mark is unique, the courts classify it by four categories, based on the correlation between the mark and the original product: (1) random or out of this world, (2) indicative, (3) expressive, or (4) basic.

Because the marks in each of these categories differ with regard to their distinctiveness, the necessities for, and degree of, legal protection provided to a particular trademark will rely upon which category it is placed within.

A random or out-of-this-world mark assumes no logical connection to the underlying product.

A suggestive mark or indicative mark brings to mind or insinuates a characteristic of the underlying well. Some implementation of imagination is required to relate the word with the underlying product. And yet the word is not completely dissimilar to the underlying product. Like arbitrary or out of this world marks, suggestive marks are essentially distinguishing and are given a high degree of protection.

A descriptive mark or expressive mark precisely describes, rather than indicates, a characteristic or feature of the underlying product (i.e. its color, odor, purpose, dimensions, or ingredients). Descriptive marks must clear this additional obstacle because they are terms that are helpful for revealing the underlying product, and giving a specific manufacturer the sole right to use the term could award an unfair advantage. A descriptive mark acquires secondary meaning when the consuming public first and foremost associates that mark with a specific producer, to a further extent than the underlying product.

The public need not be able to recognize the certain producer; only that the product or service comes from a solitary producer. When trying to decide whether a given term has acquired secondary meaning, courts will look to the following factors: (1) the amount and manner of advertising; (2) the volume of sales; (3) the length and manner of the term's use; and (4) results of consumer surveys.

A generic mark or basic mark portrays the general category to which the underlying product belongs. Generic terms are not protected by trademark law for the reason that they are simply too useful to recognize a particular product. Giving a single manufacturer control over use of the term would give that manufacturer too great a competitive advantage. Under some situations, terms that are not initially generic can become generic over time, and therefore become unprotected. A trademark characteristically becomes generic when the products or services with which it is associated have acquired considerable market supremacy or mind share. The term is legally important in that unless a company works adequately to prevent such broad use of its trademark, its intellectual property rights in the trademark may be lost. Examples include Astroturf (artificial grass), Aspirin (A.S.A. tablets, a type of pain relief medication), and Band-Aids (adhesive bandages).

What Rights do I Have as a Trademark Owner?

As an owner, trademark law protects your rights or the rights of your businesses that use the distinctive name, logo, slogan, design, or other signifiers that identify and distinguish your products and services. This protection lasts for the duration that the company uses the trademark in commerce. Trademark law is designed to address those rules that extend beyond and often confuse the uses of trademarks, service marks, and trade dress by the numerous businesses in the world today. These laws are set up to protect the names, logos, and other commercial signifiers used to distinguish specific products and services.

Keep in mind that descriptive marks meet the criteria for protection and can only be registered after they have acquired secondary meaning. Therefore, for descriptive marks, there may be a period after the preliminary use of the mark in commerce and before it acquires secondary meaning, during which it is not permitted for trademark protection. Once your trademark has achieved secondary meaning, trademark protection begins. The use of a mark normally means the actual sale of a product to the public with the mark attached.

Even though registration with the United States Patent and

Trademark Office is not required for a trademark to be protected, registration does bestow a number of benefits to the registering party. Registration conveys nationwide constructive notice that the party owns the trademark. Registration enables a party to bring an infringement suit in federal court and to potentially recuperate treble damages, attorneys fees, and other solutions.

Finally, registered trademarks can, after five years, become incontestable, at which point the sole right to use the mark is decisively established. Treble damages, in law, is a term that designates that a statute authorizes a court to triple the amount of the actual/compensatory damages to be awarded to a prevailing plaintiff, usually in order to punish the losing party for willful conduct. Treble damages are a multiple of, and not an addition to, actual damages.

Applications for registration are subject to approval by the United States Patent and Trademark Office (USPTO). The USPTO may refuse a registration on any number of reasons. As noted above, rejection of the mark does not automatically mean that it is not entitled to trademark protection; it means only that the mark is not entitled to the further benefits listed above. The rights to a trademark can be lost through abandonment, improper licensing, or assignment. The general idea is that trademark law only protects marks that are being used, and parties are not entitled to warehouse potentially useful marks.

Trademark rights can also be lost through inappropriate licensing or assignment. For example, if the use of a trademark is licensed to a franchisee, and the trademark owner does not exercise sufficient quality control or supervision, that trademark will be disregarded. Similarly, where the rights to a trademark are assigned to another party in gross, without the corresponding sale of any assets, the trademark will be canceled. The reasoning for these rules is that, under these situations, the trademark no longer serves its reason of identifying the goods of a particular provider.

The first case of definite trademark infringement, Southern v. How, was deliberated in 1618. Some common household words (aspirin, cellophane, nylon, thermos, and escalator) all started out as names for specific products but gradually became so common they became generic names.

Trademark Terminology

Abandonment of a mark

Abandonment occurs when the trademark owner stops using the mark with no intention to resume using it. Use of a mark in this context means the bona fide use of the mark made in the ordinary course of trade, and not made merely to reserve a right in a mark.

Acquiescence

It is the failure to take action against infringing parties, or otherwise indicating, implicitly or explicitly, that nothing will be done about the infringing action. Acquiescing can lead to abandonment of trademark rights. Acquiescence is the term used to describe an act of a person in intentionally standing by without raising any objection to infringement of his rights, when someone else is unintentionally and truthfully putting in his resources under the impression that the said rights actually belong to him. As a result, the person whose rights are infringed cannot make a claim anymore against the infringer or succeed in an injunction suit due to his conduct.

Action (or office action)

This is a written communication sent by the Examining Attorney from the U.S. Patent and Trademark Office requesting a response from the applicant regarding some matter pertinent to a pending application for trademark registration.

Actual confusion

This occurs when a consumer is confused to the source of goods based on similar uses of a trademark. Actual confusion is not required to prove infringement of a mark, although it is highly probative as evidence that the mark is likely to cause confusion.

Advertising, comparative

This is the use of a competitor's trademarks in advertising. Such use is permitted in the context of comparing a company's own products or services with those of their competitor, as long as the ad creates no confusion as to the source or dilution of the competitor's marks.

Advertising injury

This is a category of harm sometimes caused by trademark infringement. The significance is that some insurance policies cover litigation of a trademark dispute to the extent that the dispute falls within an advertising injury.

Aesthetic functionality

Aesthetic functionality is the widely criticized facet of the functionality doctrine, which deems as functional, and thus not trade marketable, any product design feature that is an important ingredient in the commercial success of the product. The concept of an aesthetic function that is non-trademark-related has enjoyed only limited application. In practice, aesthetic functionality has been limited to product features that serve an aesthetic purpose wholly independent of any source-identifying function.

Affirmative defenses

These are defenses to a complaint for trademark infringement that must be pleaded in the defendant's answer, or else they are waived. Examples include fraud, misuse, First Amendment, acquiescence, fair use, genericness, abandonment, and estoppel.

Affixation requirement

This refers to one of the elements that must be present in order to demonstrate that a mark is used in commerce, which is the fundamental requirement for the acquisition of rights in a mark. For a trademark to be affixed to goods, the mark should preferably be either placed on the goods themselves, or on their containers or attached tags or labels. The affixation requirement for goods may also be satisfied if the mark is significantly featured on an obvious display associated with the goods. If none of the above is practicable, the mark may be used on documents associated with the sale of the goods as a last resort. For services, a trademark is affixed if it is used in the sale or advertising of the services, as long as it is used in direct and plain reference to the services provided.

Alternative dispute resolution (ADR)

ADR is a formalized mechanism by which legal disputes can be settled outside of formal litigation. ADR may consist of mediation, arbitration, or binding arbitration. In normal cases, ADR is a lot faster and less costly than full-blown litigation. Nonetheless, that may not always be true in trademark litigation where the plaintiff often succeeds in petitioning the court for emergency intervention and a speedier court docket. Furthermore, because ADR removes many of the formalities offered by courts as required under constitutional principles of due process, it is not unusual for participants of ADR to feel as though they were not adequately heard. Whether or not ADR is advantageous for a particular situation is extremely case-dependent, and both parties need to agree to be participants.

Amendment to Allege Use

This is a special filing sometimes used for intent to use registrations in which the applicant amends the application to allege that the mark has in fact been used in commerce. The Amendment to Allege Use may be filed with the USPTO any time after filing the Intent to Use application, but before the USPTO sends a Notice of Publication.

Anti-dilution statutes

These are state and federal statutes that allow the owner of a famous trademark to prevent uses of its mark by other companies in such a way as to tarnish or blur the distinctiveness of the mark. Unlike lawsuits under a traditional trademark infringement lawsuit, the plaintiff in a dilution suit needs not prove that there is a likelihood of confusion between the famous mark and the challenged mark.

Applicant

The applicant is the person filing an application for registration of a mark under this chapter, his legal representatives, successors, or assignees.

Arbitrary marks

These are names that exist in popular vocabulary but have no logical relationship to the goods or services for which they are used. The pairing of the mark with the particular category of goods or services should appear to be random. Examples include Apple for computer, Beefeater for gin, Comet for kitchen cleaner, and Jaguar for a car. Whether a word is arbitrary or not has everything to do with the framework in which it is used. Obviously, the term "apple," used to sell a rounded edible pome fruit of a tree, is a generic term and not trademarkable.

Arbitration

A form of alternative dispute resolution in which an authorized individual sits as the arbiter of a legal dispute in lieu of a formal judicial proceeding. Arbitration may be binding or non-binding, depending on the parties. Even if arbitration is binding, appeals to a district court can still be made in some cases. Arbitration often tends to be less formal, less expensive, and faster.

Assignee

The assignee is the party to whom a trademark is being transferred in an assignment.

Assignment of trademark

An assignment is the legal transfer of ownership of any property such as a trademark or copyright from the owner to another party, who then becomes the new owner. The assignee is the person who acquires ownership, and assignor is the person who transfers ownership rights.

Assignment, in gross

Assignment of a mark without the necessary transfer of goodwill associated with the mark. Such assignments are invalid and result in abandonment of the trademark. If so, the person to whom the mark was assigned will no longer have the benefit of the assignor's earlier first use date to establish priority.

Assumed name

Also known as a trade name or corporate name, it is the name under which a company conducts its business. Whereas an assumed name identifies the business itself, trademarks identify goods or services. An assumed name can also be a trademark if it meets the requirements of a trademark.

Bad faith (bad intent)

Bad faith is a mental state characterized by an intent to deceive consumers by using a competitor's trademark or one that is confusingly similar to it. Bad faith is not required to find trademark infringement or dilution.

Blackout period

This is the period in which an Intent to Use trademark applicant is prohibited from filing an Amendment to Allege Use or a Statement of Use. This period begins once the mark is published in the *Official Gazette*, and continues until the USPTO issues a Notice of Allowance.

Balance of harms

This occurs prior to ordering injunctive relief, which is an equitable remedy, the court must weigh the harm to the defendant if the injunction is imposed against the harm to the plaintiff if no injunction is ordered.

Blurring

Blurring is one of the two ways a famous trademark can be diluted. Particularly, blurring occurs where someone uses a mark which takes away some of the strength of the famous mark by using it in a different context. While this may not confuse consumers, it may damage the famous mark's ability to exclusively and characteristically identify a source of goods and services.

Book titles, protection of

Book titles are generally not protected under trademark law unless they are part of a series.

Brand name

The popular vernacular for a lingual trademark, typically used in conjunction with goods. Even though a brand name is always a trademark, a trademark is not always a brand name, since a trademark may be a sound, a color, product packaging, etc.

Certification mark

This is a symbol used to identify goods or services that meet certain criteria such as quality ratings or content levels.

Coined terms (fanciful terms)

These are terms that are invented for the sole purpose of serving as trademarks.

Collective mark

A collective mark is a symbol used by members of a group to identify their association with the group, such as a union, co-op, or trade or professional associations.

Colors, protection of

Colors, whether one or a combination of them, can be protected under trademark law if the colors otherwise meet the definition of a trademark. In a 1995 case, Qualitex v. Co. v. Jacobson Prods. Co., 514 U.S. 159, the Supreme court rejected earlier lower court decisions that had refused to protect colors as trademarks. Those earlier decisions maintained that businesses would soon deplete the limited supply of colors available, and unjustly prevent others from entering the marketplace, thus generating an undesirable monopoly. The Court in Qualitex pointed out that there are countless shades of colors available, thereby rejecting the depletion of colors theory.

Combined application

This is an application for trademark registration containing multiple international classes. Each class costs $245 to register, although all the classes can be applied for on one application.

Comparative advertising

Comparative advertising is the use of another company's trademark to compare that company's products with its own. Whether or not comparative advertising qualifies as trademark infringement or those bodies of law govern dilution.

Common law

A law originating from court decisions and refined through prior court precedents, as distinguished from law created by the legislative branch of government such as statutes. Common law is also referred to as court-made law.

Concurrent use

Used by two or more persons of the same mark in connection with the same or similar products or services, usually limited by geographic boundaries.

Concurrent use registration

A federal registration, which delineates certain limitations on the use of a mark due to the concurrent use of a similar mark. Usually speaking, the first of two companies to use a mark is entitled to nationwide registration rights, except for the specific geographic area in which the second company is using the mark, even if the first user has not used the mark nationwide.

Conflicts between trademarks

Conflicts between trademarks can occur due to two marks being similar to each other in such a way that consumers are likely to be confused as to which is which.

Constructive use

Constructive use is where use of a trademark is deemed to have occurred even without actual use, pursuant to a statute.

Copyrights, generally

Ownership rights in expressive works (not ideas), granting the owner exclusive control over distribution, display, copying, performance, and adaptation of those works. The Copyright Office is the umbrella of the Library of Congress that governs the registration of copyrighted works.

Corporate name

Also known as a trade name, it is the name under which a company conducts its business. Whereas a corporate name identifies the business itself, trademarks identify goods or services.

Counterfeit Goods:

Goods bearing a trademark that is either identical with, or substantially indistinguishable from, a federally registered marks. While infringement of a trademark requires confusing resemblance between marks, in spite of the intent of the infringer, counterfeiting can only occur when the perpetrator knowingly used the counterfeit mark with an intent to traffic in the goods bearing the mark.

Damages

Damages are monetary amount awarded to the plaintiff by the court in order to compensate the plaintiff for actual injury sustained by the actions of the defendant. In trademark cases, the basis of damages is typically the plaintiff's lost profits or defendant's profits as a result of the infringing activity, and may include prejudgment interest.

Database, trademark

Many businesses now provide over the Internet databases of existing and pending trademarks, which the user can search, usually for a very reasonable fee. The services vary in their timeliness and whether or not state trademark registrations are available. The only free database is maintained by the U.S. Patent and Trademark Office (USPTO) itself, and can be accessed on the Internet at **http://www.USPTO.GOV/tmdb/index.html**.

Date of first use

This refers to the date a mark was first used anywhere. In the United States, the first to use a mark generally has priority and can exclude all subsequent users of identical or confusingly similar marks.

Date of first use in commerce

To secure a date of first use in commerce, the mark owner must use the mark in trade in a manner that allows consumers to rely on it to identify and discriminate between the user's goods or services and those of competitors'. In addition, since the authority for the Trademark Act is based on the interstate commerce clause, the user must also demonstrate use in interstate commerce in order to obtain a federal registration.

Deceptive marks

These are marks that cannot be registered as trademarks because they mischaracterize or mislead consumers as to the underlying product. The usual test for determining whether or not a mark is deceptive is: (1) the mark misrepresents the character, quality, function, composition, or use of the underlying product; (2) purchasers are likely to believe the misrepresentation actually describes the goods; and (3) purchasers are likely to rely upon the misrepresentation in making their purchasing decision.

Depository libraries

These are selected public libraries that house the CASSIS, a powerful database containing all existing and pending federal trademarks maintained by the USPTO, available at all Patent and Trademark Depository Libraries. CASSIS allows simple and complex searching, and search results can be reformatted and exported. Federal registrations often include terms disclaimed as being generic.

Description of goods or services

A description of goods or services is required in all applications for federal trademark registration.

Descriptive marks

Descriptive marks refer to trademarks that describe the ingredients, qualities, features, purpose, or characteristics of a product or service.

De facto secondary meaning

De facto secondary meaning exists where an interest in the public good overrides the protection of a mark that otherwise serves to identify the source for consumers and has acquired secondary meaning. De facto secondary meaning also exists when a mark is generic or functional.

Defenses to dilution

The following provide a bar or defense to a claim of trademark dilution: the mark used is a federally registered trademark; it only bars claims of dilution brought under state or common law, not those under federal law; use of a famous mark by another person in comparative advertising to recognize competing goods or services; noncommercial use of a mark; and all forms of news reporting and news commentary.

Distinctiveness

Distinctiveness refers to the ability of a mark to allow the relevant consuming public to discriminate the source of a product or service. Distinctiveness is a prerequisite to trademark registration on the Principal Register. Fanciful, arbitrary, and suggestive marks are inherently distinctive, while descriptive marks are not distinctive unless used extensively enough to develop a certain level of market awareness, called secondary meaning.

Documenting first use

Because trademark rights in the United States are on a first-to-use basis, it is important to document the first date you use a mark. Taking a dated photograph of the goods bearing the mark may do this or keeping the original advertising if it shows the date the advertisement ran. You should also keep records of the first sale of goods or services made using the mark. This may include a bill of sale or invoice.

Domain name

A component of an Internet address (URL), which is composed of a top-level domain such as .com or .net and a second level domain, which is the part the domain name owner gets to make up.

Domestic representative

A resident of the United States to whom service of process may be sent regarding the trademark. Foreign applicants for trademark registration are required to have a domestic representative unless an attorney in the United States also represents them.

Encircled R (the ®, symbol)

The encircled R, or ®, is a symbol that designates a specific trade or service mark as a federally registered trademark under the Trademark Act. In order to use this symbol, a mark must be currently registered on either the Principle or Supplemental Registers maintained by the USPTO. Willful use of the encircled R on a non-registered mark may jeopardize future availability of registration status with the USPTO, and may be evidence of bad intent, which is frowned upon by the courts.

Estoppel

Estoppel is a legal term for stopping certain outcomes demanded by a party to a lawsuit. In trademark litigation, the plaintiff is said to be estopped from claiming infringement if plaintiff's actions, or lack thereof, indicated authorization of defendant's use of the trademark (acquiescence).

Examination (of trademark application)

All applications for trademark registration in the United States must undergo an extensive examination process, which is conducted by trademark examiners at the USPTO.

Exclusive license

An exclusive license is an agreement between a trademark owner and one other party that permits the other party to make certain use of the trademark, with the understanding that the trademark owner will not permit other such uses.

Exclusive licensee

An exclusive licensee is the party to whom a trademark owner grants an exclusive license to use a trademark.

Exclusive licensor

This refers to the trademark owner who is licensing its trademark for exclusive use by one other company.

Exclusive ownership

This refers to ownership in a mark, which is free of any claim of right by any other party.

Exclusive rights

Exclusive rights are rights granted to an owner of a trade or service mark which permit the owner to use a mark, and to exclude all others from using the same or a similar mark in a similar manner.

Famous mark

A famous mark commands a wide degree of familiarity such that it receives special protection under the Federal Trademark Dilution Act.

Filing date, obtaining

The filing date is the date in which an application for federal trademark registration is accepted into the USPTO.

First use date

This is the date a mark was first used anywhere. In the United States, the first person to use a mark has precedence and can exclude all following users of identical or confusingly comparable marks. For this reason, it is vital to document the date of first use of a mark. This may be done by taking a dated photograph of the goods bearing the mark or keeping the original advertising if it shows the date that the ad ran.

Forbidden marks

These are marks that cannot accept protection through the courts nor registration with the U.S. Patent and Trademark Office. They include generic marks; immoral, disparaging, or reprehensible marks; marks which are primarily functional; marks consisting of a living person's name, portrait or signature, unless written permission has been granted; deceptive marks, and marks consisting of a deceased President's name, unless that President's spouse has granted written permission or is no longer alive.

Fraud

Fraud occurs when the mark owner knowingly made a false representation to the USPTO.

Functionality doctrine (utilitarian functionality)

According to this doctrine, the functional features of a trademark, or those features having primarily a utilitarian purpose, are not granted protection. Where product essentials such as shape, color, or design are vital to improve the sales future of a product, or because the product requires the trademarked element to function optimally, then that feature is not protected by trademark law.

Generic marks

These are words or symbols that describe the product or service itself as a category, rather than distinguish between competing versions of the product or service.

Genericized trademark

Also known as a generic trade mark or proprietary eponym is a trademark or brand name that has become the colloquial or generic description for, or synonymous with, a particular class of product or service.

Geographical territory

The geographical territory is the territory in which one uses a mark. Use in a territory generally determines the extent of trademark rights granted to the user.

Goodwill

An intangible reward for businesses once they generate name recognition and establish public confidence in their goods or services. When this happens, consumers want to return to that business for repeat purchases.

Goodwill, assignment without

Assignment or transfer of a trademark must occur in conjunction with the transfer of goodwill represented by that mark, or else the assignment is invalid. Additionally, if assignment occurs without goodwill, the trademark is effectively abandoned characteristically. It is the assignee's rights in the mark that are abandoned, but sometimes it is the assignor that abandons its rights.

Grammatical rules when using marks

Failure to use the proper grammatical rules when using a trademark may result in the mark becoming generic, and thereby losing all its protection. Specifically, it is very important to always use the mark as if it were an adjective, and never use it as a noun.

Grounds for cancellation

Cancellation of a trademark registration can occur within the first five years of registration for any reason that the mark could have been precluded from registration in the first place. Particularly that includes: likelihood of confusion with petitioner's previously used or registered mark, fraud, descriptiveness, genericness, abandonment, misrepresentation, and deceptiveness. However, fair use, trademark misuse, unfair competition, or violation of anti-trust laws are generally not considered valid grounds for cancellation.

Identifying source

Identifying the source of a product or service for the consuming public is the primary objective of trademark law. The Trademark Act grants exclusive rights only to those trademarks enabling a consumer to discriminate between different brands of goods and services. The consumer need not be able to discern the precise manufacturer or service provider by company name.

Immoral marks (scandalous marks)

A mark consisting of immoral or scandalous matter cannot be federally registered. Courts have defined scandalous marks to include marks giving offense to the conscience or moral feelings, exciting reprobation, or calling out condemnation for a substantial composite of the general public.

Incontestability status

A benefit granted to owners of federal trademark registrations, allowing them to prohibit challenges pertaining to the owner's exclusive rights in a mark. Incontestability can help prevent attacks on the basis that the mark is confusingly similar to another mark, that it is functional, or that it lacks secondary meaning. Incontestability status does not mean a mark is attack-proof.

Ingredients, protection of

As long as an ingredient in a product is also used as a trademark, it is worthy of trademark protection.

In gross assignment

Assignment of a mark without the necessary transfer of goodwill associated with the mark. Such assignments are invalid and can result in abandonment of the trademark.

Inherent distinctiveness

A mark can be inherently distinctive, or can acquire distinctiveness over time. Marks that are inherently distinctive are those with the ability upon being used the very first time to communicate to the consumer that the mark is identifying the basis of the product as opposed to describing the product itself.

Intellectual property

The term used to identify a form of property rights granted to intangible creations of the mind. There are distinct varieties of intellectual property, including trademarks, copyrights, patents, trade secrets, and publicity rights. Each state protects intellectual property in its own way, if at all.

Intent to Use (ITU) application

This is an application for a federal registration made to the USPTO for a trademark that is not yet being used. ITU applications secure trademark rights prior to actually using the mark. It allows companies the opportunity to see if the USPTO will register the mark without having to invest in the marketing and promotion of the mark in the event that the mark is rejected. It also secures an early priority date.

International class

An international class is a number associated with a category of goods or services into which a trademark may be assigned for the purposes of a trademark registration.

International Trade Commission (ITC)

The ITC can help halt the importation of counterfeit goods by issuing a temporary or permanent exclusion order. The ITC has its own rules of practice and detection, and the Commission participates as a party and conducts its own discovery. The ITC can grant temporary relief such as injunctions and restraining orders that can be granted under the Federal Rules of Civil Procedure.

Invalid assignment

Any assignment of a trademark is invalid if the assignment of the mark is made without assignment of the goodwill associated with the mark. If a mark is invalidly assigned, the usual result is that the company that purchased the mark, the assignee, is deprived of the benefit of the early priority date of the assignor, and must instead start all over with a new priority date beginning when the assignee begins using the mark in commerce.

Junior user

The second or subsequent user of a mark who may or may not have rights in the mark, depending on whether the mark is being used in the same territory as the senior (first) user.

Labels, trademark protection of

Labels on goods can be protected under trademark law if the feature on the label for which trademark protection is claimed identifies the source for consumers, and if such features are not functional.

Legal strength of a trademark

Strength of a mark can be measured on two different levels: marketing strength and legal strength.

Letters, trademark protection of

Alphabetic and alphanumeric characters can be protected under trademark law, and indeed compose the most common form of trademark, otherwise known as textual or lingual marks.

License

A license is an agreement between a trademark owner and one or more parties that allows the other parties to make limited, specified use of the trademark in question.

Licensee

The party to whom a trademark owner grants a license to use a trademark.

Licensor

The trademark owner who is licensing a trademark to the trademark licensee(s).

Lingual marks

These are trademarks in the form of either words or phrases and are the most widely used kinds of marks.

Mark

Mark refers to any trademark, service mark, certification mark, or collective mark.

Market survey

A market survey is research conducted by an independent firm and used to support arguments before the USPTO or civil courts when trying to prove various aspects of trademark viability.

Misspelled words as marks

Often, business owners choose misspelled words that are phonetically similar to the correctly spelled word, in hopes of adding distinctiveness, or even perhaps as a marketing ploy.

Misuse of trademark 11.49

Misuse of trademark 11.49 refers to an affirmative defense to trademark infringement. Misuse occurs when the trademark owner uses the mark in violation of the law, such as canceling a trademark license on the basis of illegal discrimination.

Monopoly

Monopoly refers to a privilege vested in one or more parties consisting of the exclusive right to carry on a particular business or trade. In the case of trademark law, a monopoly specifically references the exclusive right to use a word, symbol, sound or trade dress, etc., in association with a particular kind of good or service.

Multiple-class application

An application for federal trademark registration in which the applicant seeks registration for more than one international class. The registrant must pay an additional registration fee for each class applied for.

Musical notation, trademark protection of

Musical notes appearing with or without a staff is protected as long as they function as proper trademarks.

Naked assignment

This refers to an assignment of a mark without the necessary transfer of goodwill associated with the mark. Such assignments are invalid and may result in abandonment of the trademark.

Naked license

Naked license is the licensing of a trademark without the necessary controls over the use of the mark.

Name reservation

Name reservation is registering the name of a business with the state in order to reserve that name for the business owner. Most states will reserve a name that is not an exact duplicate of an existing name, with no attention given to confusingly similar names that may infringe existing trademarks.

Nationwide priority

Nationwide priority is an exception to the common law rule that the first person to use a mark in a territory has priority in that territory. A federal trademark registration allows whoever is first to register a mark to have priority in any territory in which the mark is not already being used. Without federal registration, or nationwide priority, a trademark owner can be the first to use a mark in one area of the country, but a junior user is free to use the original owner's mark in a different area of the country.

Natural expansion

Natural expansion is a doctrine whereby rights in a trademark are granted based on expected use rather than actual use.

Non-exclusive license

This is a form of trademark license, which grants the person, licensed (i.e. licensee) something other than an exclusive entitlement to the mark.

Notice

A notice of trademark rights is given by use of the symbols, ™, ℠, or ®, or by phrases such as "XYZ Company is the registered owner of the trademark ABC," or "Reg. U.S. Pat. Off."

Notice of publication

A notice sent to the applicant of a pending trademark registration that their trademark has been approved by the trademark examiners.

Official Gazette

The short name for *The Official Gazette of the United States Patent and Trademark Office*. It is a weekly publication containing information about all pending trademarks, changes to existing marks, and trademark renewals.

Ordinary designs, distinctiveness of

Designs ordinary or commonplace, such as simple lines or geometric figures, are not inherently distinctive, but may become distinctive through use. Marks not distinctive cannot be registered on the Principle Register until they acquire secondary meaning.

Ownership, acquisition of

In the U.S., ownership rights in a trademark are commonly acquired by being the first to use a mark in trade as a source discriminator.

Ornamentation

This refers to an attribute of a product, which may not be protected under trademark law. Under the aesthetic functionality doctrine, those design characteristics of a product that are mere ornamentation (i.e. aesthetically pleasing and helping to improve the sale of a product, but not primarily assisting in distinguishing goods from a competitor's) cannot receive trademark protection.

Packaging, trademark protection of W10, 14

Protection is available for packaging as long as the elements claimed for trademark protection meet the requirements of a trademark. The elements that are protected may include the shape and color or overall coordination of these elements.

Parallel imports (gray-market goods)

These are goods that are not authorized for importation into the United States. These goods were legitimately sold outside the United States with the approval of the manufacturer but were not supposed to be resold back into the United States. The importers of gray-market goods are attempting to benefit from the higher prices such goods command within the United States as compared to the country in which they were originally sold.

Patent and Trademark Office

The United States Patent and Trademark Office, or USPTO, is the administrative body that administers the registration and cancellation of trademarks and patents on the Principal and Supplemental Register.

Patent attorney

It is not necessary to have a patent attorney doing trademark-related work. A patent attorney is typically an attorney with an engineering or other scientific degree who is specially licensed to handle patent matters before the USPTO.

Personal names, trademark protection of

Traditionally, courts have been reluctant to make illegal the use of one's own name in business, even when another business exists by the same name. Courts would try to fashion injunctions to be as slight as possible to authorize use of a personal name. Lately, courts have become more and more insensitive to any prohibition on using one's own name, where such use creates a probability of confusion for consumers.

Petitioner

The petitioner is the party to a cancellation proceeding who seeks to cancel the federal registration of a trademark held by the registrant in such an action.

Physical features, protection of

Shapes or physical features of products or their containers may receive trademark protection if distinctive and non-functional.

Presidents' names, trademark protection for

The Lanham Act specifically prohibits use of a U.S. president's name as a trademark, if the president is alive and has not given express written consent. If the president is deceased, but the president's spouse is still alive, written consent must be obtained from the spouse before the president's name may be used. If the president is deceased and their spouse is no longer living, there name may be trademarked.

Primarily geographically descriptive 2.20

A term used in the manner of a trademark that conveys to the consumer a geographical connotation primarily or immediately. If the consumer is likely to believe that the underlying goods or services come from that location, and that location is the geographic origin of the underlying goods or services, then the mark is primarily geographically descriptive and can be registered on the Supplemental Register, or on the Principal Register if the mark owner can demonstrate secondary meaning.

Principal Register

This is the primary registry of trademarks maintained by the USPTO. In order to qualify for registration on the Principal Register, a trademark must be distinctive and currently in use. Trademarks that qualify for Principal Register registration receive all the benefits of registration, whereas those registered on the Supplemental Register do not.

Priority date

The priority date is the date that determines who will triumph in a trademark infringement lawsuit. In the United States, the priority date is, in general, the date a trademark was first used. In most other countries, the priority date is based on whoever is first to file for a trademark registration.

Prior registration

Prior registration is a trademark registration that was filed before another. In most countries other than the United States, the first to register a trademark has the right to exclude others from using that mark in a similar manner.

Product design

Product design consists of the variety of elements, which constitute the configuration of the product. Product configurations are protected as long as they are distinguishing and operate like a trademark.

Protest letter

A protest letter is written to the USPTO in order to protest the registration of a mark.

Publication of trademark (publication period)

Once the Trademark Examining Attorney has approved a mark; the mark is published in the *Official Gazette* for three months. The reason of publication is to inform existing mark owners of potentially infringing marks and give them a chance to respond with a protest letter.

Quality assurance in licensing

Quality assurance is a vital part of trademark licensing, because where there is unfettered use of a mark by another party, a trademark will lose its ability to identify a single source.

Recording registration with U.S. Customs

Recording a trademark allows United States Customs to interdict the importation of counterfeit goods, goods with infringing marks, and gray-market goods.

Register, Principal

This is the primary registry of trademarks maintained by the USPTO. In order to meet the criteria for registration on the Principal Register, a trademark must be distinctive and presently in use. Trademarks that qualify for Principal Register registration receive all the benefits of registration, whereas those registered on the Supplemental Register do not.

Register, Supplemental

The Supplemental Register is a secondary list of registered marks preserved by the USPTO. Marks on the Supplemental Register do not qualify for registration on the Principal Register, and as such, these marks do not receive the many benefits of registration available on the Principal Register.

Registrant

Registrant includes the person to whom the registration of a mark under this chapter is issued, and the registrant's legal representatives, successors, or assignees.

Registration Symbol

The ® is a symbol signifying federal trademark registration. The federal registration symbol is used once a mark (a trademark or service mark) is actually registered with the USPTO.

Remedies for infringement

Depending on one's perspective, a remedy may either be the penalty applied when found liable for infringement or dilution of a trademark, or the relief that the trademark owner may obtain under such circumstances. Remedies available include: injunctive relief to stop use of the mark, monetary relief, a bar on importation, cancellation of trademark registration, criminal indictment, a declaratory judgment, or other equitable relief as the court may see fit.

Response

A response is a reply from a trademark applicant to the USPTO after the USPTO has sent the applicant an initial refusal of trademark registration. A response is due after six months of receiving the office action, or else the application will be deemed abandoned.

Secondary meaning

An awareness on the part of the applicable consuming public that a mark recognizes a specific good or service and is not limited to its common, or primary, meaning. Secondary meaning is acquired only after revealing the term as a brand identifier after widespread advertising. Descriptive marks and surnames must acquire secondary meaning in order to become registered or to be protected as a trademark.

Service mark

A service mark is similar to a trademark but distinguishes services rather than tangible products. The service mark can be a word, a symbol, a design, or some combination of those elements. In some countries, a service mark could also be a sound, color, or even texture.

Shapes, trademark protection of 1.1

Product shapes are capable of trademark protection under the rapidly expanding doctrine of trade dress as long as the shape meets the requirements of a trademark and is not a functional feature of the underlying product.

Similarity of marks

Similar marks cannot coexist as trademarks if they are similar in such a way that is likely to cause consumers to be confused as to the source of the products using such marks.

Slogans, trademark protection of1.1, 2.22

Slogans are capable of attaining trademark protection as long as they meet the requirements of a trademark. Nevertheless, since slogans often are used as marketing instruments to describe the underlying product or service, they are almost always descriptive and lack inherent uniqueness. Once they are used at length enough in the marketplace to obtain secondary meaning, they may be registered.

Smells, trademark protection of1.1

Trademark protection exists for smells to the extent that they meet the requirements of a trademark.

Sounds, trademark protection of

Trademark protection exists for any sounds or musical compositions to the extent that such music meets the requirements of a trademark. A famous example is the three notes heard along with the NBC peacock.

Specimen

Specimens are items that serve as evidence for actual use of a mark. The USPTO requires all trademark applicants to submit three specimens of the trademark as it is used in commerce. The specimens can be the same or different.

State versus federal trademark

State trademarks are typically used exclusively in intrastate commerce, while a federal mark must be used in interstate commerce in order to be registered.

Strength of mark

Strength of a mark can be measured on two different levels: marketing strength and legal strength. Words that closely describe the underlying good or service they stand for have fervent marketing potential, since such marks instantaneously communicate to customers what the product actually is or what it does.

Suggestive terms

Suggestive trademarks propose rather than describe qualities of the underlying good or service. "Suggestive" and "descriptive" are not equally exclusive, since there must be some description in almost any suggestion.

Surnames, trademark protection of

Trademarks consisting of a person's own last name are generally not protected under trademark law unless the mark has acquired secondary meaning. In some instances, a name may not require secondary meaning in order to receive protection. That occurs when the surname also describes some other thing, such as Bird, King, or Flowers.

Symbols, protection of

Trademarks can be any symbol as long as the symbol meets the requirements of trademarks. Logos are symbols that are not lingual marks, and they must be registered as design trademarks.

Tarnishment

Tarnishment is one of the two ways a famous trademark can be weakened. Specifically, tarnishment occurs when someone uses a mark, which set off the famous mark to be connected with lesser quality products or seen in an unpleasant context.

Telephone numbers, protection of

As long as a telephone number meets the requirements of a trademark (i.e. that consumers can rely upon it to differentiate the trademark owner's goods or services from those of competitors), then it can receive all the protections supplied by trademark and dilution law. In general, protection for phone numbers is sought after for those numbers that are converted to a significant word, such as in the case of "Dial D-O-C-T-O-R-S" in which a court enjoined another company's use of the same phrase outside of the region in which the phone number was first secured.

TM symbol 4.13

The TM symbol used next to a trademark provides notice to the world that a company claims trademark rights in that mark. Companies can use the TM symbol on any mark, which operates to identify that company's goods, and the SM symbol on any mark, which serves to recognize that company's services. There is no need to have a federal or state registration prior to using the TM or SM symbols. Conversely, use of the © symbol does require a federal registration.

Trade dress (product design)

Trade dress consists of the variety of elements in which a product is packaged or a service is presented. The elements that are protected may include the shape, color, or overall packaging of goods, the displays attending goods, and even the decor or environment in which a service is provided. However, only those elements that were designed specifically to promote the product are protected, not the functional features of trade dress that have a utilitarian purpose.

Trademark

A trademark identifies and discriminates between goods, whether or not distinctively, from those manufactured or sold by others. In order to qualify as a trademark, the mark must be used in federally regulated commerce, and the mark must be unique. The uniqueness requirement means that a mark cannot describe the underlying product, or if it does explain the product, the mark must have been used comprehensively enough in commerce to obtain a particular level of market recognition.

Trademark misuse

A theoretical basis for canceling a trademark. Although purely speculative at this point, some legal scholars have suggested that a trademark registrant should lose their rights if they engage in abusive tactics that violate the boundaries of fair competition.

Trademark search

An investigation to uncover any potential conflicts between a proposed mark and an existing one.

Trade name

Also known as an assumed name or corporate name, it is the name under which a company conducts its business. Whereas a trade name identifies the business itself, trademarks identify goods or services. A trade name can also serve as a trademark if it meets the requirements of a trademark.

Transferee

A transferee is the party who acquires rights in an assignment or transfer of trademark rights.

Transferor

The party who conveys rights to the transferee in the transfer or assignment of trademarks.

Types of marks

The words "trademark" or "mark" are used in a universal manner to denote any kind of mark such as a certification mark, collective mark, service mark, or trademark. Service mark is used in association with the sale of services, while trademark is used in association with the sale of goods. Certification marks are used to identify a level of quality or that specific standards have been met, and collective marks are used to distinguish associations of companies or organizations. Any such mark can consist of a symbol, smell, sound, phrase, or packaging, if it is used to identify the thing about which it is supposed to make a distinction.

United States Customs Bureau

United States Customs officials can insist on disclosure of the identity of any trademark on imported goods and under certain situations can seize goods bearing infringing marks. Congress has sanctioned the Customs Bureau's involvement in thwarting the importation of counterfeit goods, gray market goods, and goods bearing infringing trademarks.

United States Patent and Trademark Office (USPTO)

The federal agency presiding over the registration and maintenance of patents and federal trademarks. While attorneys must have an additional license to practice patent law before the USPTO, no such requirement exists for the practice of trademark law before this body.

Use, proper 4.12

To use a mark properly, the trademark owner should: always use the mark as an adjective of the underlying product rather than as a noun, as in "People prefer ARM STRONG brand steaks" rather than "People prefer ARMSTRONG"; italicize, underline, capitalize, or boldface the mark when it appears in text, in order to set it apart from the generic word for the product; affix the mark to the goods or services, and provide proper notice of trademark rights.

Utilitarian functionality

According to this doctrine, the functional features of a trademark, or those features having primarily a utilitarian purpose, are not granted protection. When product elements such as shape, color, or design are necessary to improve the sales of a product, or when the product requires the trademarked element to function optimally, then trademark law does not protect that feature.

Validity of trademark 15.3

The validity of a trademark is judged primarily by its ability to identify for consumers the source of a good or service and distinguish it from other brands. However, there are some instances where a mark serves this function perfectly well, but is still invalid as a trademark.

Warehousing of trademarks

This refers to preservation of rights in a mark by making periodic, "token use" over time, with no present intent to commercially exploit the mark. Prior to the 1988 revision of the Trademark Act in which Intent to Use applications became available, warehousing was used to secure early priority rights in a mark without actually using the mark. At present, warehousing is still used to circumvent the law of trademark abandonment, which states that a mark is abandoned, and thus no longer able to protect, when the owner discontinues its use with no intent to resume use in the reasonably foreseeable future.

Willful infringement

This is trademark infringement that occurs when the user of a mark knows or should have known that the mark was already being used. The consequence of willful infringement is that the defendant is liable for monetary damages, whereas an innocent infringer can only be forced to stop using the mark.

Words, trademark protection of

Words are the most common type of trademark, and receive protection as long as they meet the requirements of a trademark. Depending on the meaning of the word or phrase, these marks have more or less legal strength.

Trademark Symbols

The Pillsbury Doughboy is a famous registered trademark. A trademark is a special design or word that is used to represent a service or product.

Building designs can also serve as trademarks or service marks. For example, the McDonald's Arches are a famous design registered to McDonald's Corporation for restaurant services. Other registered trademarks include the Puma Company's design and the Ford emblem.

Pictures or drawings of a scene or character, like the Pink Panther (registered trademark of the Corning Company) or MSN's Butterfly (registered trademark of Microsoft), are often used as trademarks or service marks.

Apple's iPod is a registered product shape, a form of trademark. A product or container shape can also function as an identification and therefore can be an enforceable trademark.

Can a sound be trademarked?

Yes, a sound can also be a trademark or a service mark. The three-tone chime of NBC has been registered as a service mark. Sound trademarks were in the news recently when Harley-Davidson declared that it was attempting to register the exhaust sound of a Harley-Davidson motorcycle.

A trademark also might be a combination of letters and a design, such as IBM or Silicon Graphics.

Logos are almost certainly the next most common form of mark. A logo can be depicted as a design that becomes a mark when used in close relationship with the goods or services being marketed. The logo mark does not have to be complicated; it only needs to differentiate goods and services sold under the mark from other goods and services. Dunkin' Donuts' trademarked label is an example of this.

Phrases or taglines can also be converted into trademarks:

- *"Don't leave home without it"* — American Express

- *"The greatest show on earth"* — Ringling Bros. Barnum & Bailey Circus

- *"Everywhere you want to be"* — Visa

- *"Just do it"* — Nike

Essential Concepts

What is the essential concept of trademarks and trademark laws?

The essential purpose of a trademark is to absolutely identify the commercial source or origin of products or services (i.e. that a trademark, properly called, designates source or serves as a badge of origin). The use of a trademark in this way is known as trademark use.

Terms such as "mark," "brand," and "logo" are sometimes used as tradeoffs with "trademark." On the other hand, the terms "brands" and "branding" raise distinct theoretical issues and are normally more suitable for use in a marketing or advertising context.

International Trademark Laws

How the international trademark laws work and what they cover compared to American laws, as well as how the differing conceptions of trademark rights through a consideration of trademark protections established outside the United States, are included in the Paris Convention, the TRIPs Agreement, the

Madrid System, and European Union regulations. The problems with international trademark laws include cyber-squatting, and country-code top-level domains, ICANN, the Uniform Domain Name Dispute Resolution Process (UDRP), and the reports of the two WIPO Internet Domain Name Processes.

The Madrid System and the Paris Convention

The convention stated that two independent treaties run registration of trademarks in numerous jurisdictions around the world: the Madrid Agreement and the Madrid Protocol. Despite its name, the Protocol is an unconnected treaty and not a "protocol" to the Agreement. Together, the Agreement and the Protocol are known as the Madrid System for the International Registration of Marks, or the Madrid System. Together they constitute the Madrid Union, which is a Special Union under Article 19 of the Paris Convention. The Madrid System is centrally managed by the International Bureau of the World Intellectual Property Organization (WIPO) for obtaining a bundle of trademark registrations in separate jurisdictions, creating a basis for an "international registration" of marks.

The Collection of Laws for Electronic Access (CLEA)

The Collection of Laws for Electronic Access (CLEA) is an electronic database providing access to intellectual property legislation from a wide range of countries and regions as well as to treaties on intellectual property. This information resource is made available by WIPO free of charge to all interested parties, including researchers, legal professionals, students, and administrators.

Chapter 10

History of Trademarks

"People recognize intellectual property the same way they recognize real estate. People understand what property is. But it's a new kind of property, and so the understanding uses new control surfaces. It uses a new way of defining the property."

Michael Nesmith

Trademark history goes back quite a ways. The marking of goods for various purposes, including differentiating them from those of other traders, dates back to ancient times. In the same way, the existence of rules governing the use of such marks goes back to the medieval craft guilds.

From the beginning of time and the use of cave paintings to the stone seals of some 5,000 years ago, trademarks have been used to designate the property of one person or tribe from another. In ancient times the Greeks, Romans, and Egyptians all used a form of trademark, either markings or stamps to indicate which of them had made a certain item. Not only did this lead to rewards for those who made the items, but it also allowed for blame when the items failed.

It was only in the 19th century that people began to think of marks, which had become distinctive of a trader's goods and so attracted valuable goodwill, as a type of property. In the middle of that century, the right to take action in the courts against infringement of a trademark came about, even when there was no intention to deceive on the part of the infringer.

Livestock from the Stone Age to the old West were branded to depict ownership. Masons in Egypt more than 6,000 years ago used stonecutter signs and quarry marks to show who completed the work. It has always been commonplace in the practice of creating goods to certify the origin with a graphic design or mark, and if the quality was good that mark brought more prestige to the creator.

Chapter 11

Trademark Search Logistics

"A great trademark is appropriate, dynamic, distinctive, memorable and unique."

Primo Angel

A trademark search seeks to establish if there is a conflict with another's trademark. The search is performed without taking any pointless action that may place any prior trademark owner on notice of an infringement problem. A search also helps circumvent filing a trademark application that will not issue. Whether to conduct a trademark search is a business decision that should be based on the uniqueness of the trademark and whether the trademark will in reality be in use within nine months of filing the application.

How to Search for Trademarks

A search of the federal trademark records can be conducted somewhat rapidly. A more extensive search of federal, state, and common law trademarks can be conducted in days. Note though, that no trademark search can be totally complete. Because trademark rights are based on use, it is recommended to first conduct a comprehensive search to determine if someone else is using the same or similar name. Nevertheless, unlike a business selling products or services, a traditional trademark search service may not be enough for a performer or band. Trademark searches provide the information you need about the availability of your proposed mark and can save a lot of time and money in the future.

When searching, be familiar with your objective. Preferably, you should search all registered and unregistered trademarks, of which there are millions. Know that you are searching for trademarks that sound like, look like, or mean the same thing as your planned trademark. Begin your search with the free trademark database on the USPTO's Web site. The USPTO's database consists of all registered marks and all marks for which registration is pending. Furthermore, besides searching for registered or pending trademarks on the USPTO's Web site, search the Internet casually for unregistered trademarks. If possible, visit your local Patent and Trademark Depository Library (PTDL) and use their research materials. A list of PTDLS (and there is at least one in every state) is accessible from the USPTO's home page. Think about using a professional search service. You can order a complete search of registered and unregistered marks through Trademark Express.

After Searching, What Now?

What if you find that someone already has the rights to a trademark, or one that is closely related to yours? There are ways to help you still get your trademark complete whether someone has the trademark or one that is closely related to it. Go ahead and use your selection if, after your search, you determine that your proposed trademark is not exactly the same as or similar to a trademark that belongs to someone else. Begin taking steps to protect your trademark as well. If your search does turn up possible conflicts, determine whether customer confusion is likely to occur if you use your planned trademark. Customer confusion is unlikely if the products or services do not compete with each other and are not marketed through the same means. If you are sure customer confusion is not likely, and your proposed trademark does not staunchly resemble a famous trademark, you may decide to go ahead and use the trademark.

Zildjian, known for its cymbals and gongs, holds one of the oldest continuously used trademarks in the U.S.

Chapter 12

The Internet and Names for Trademark Use

" Let superiority be your trademark."

Orison Swett Marden

The booming industry of the Internet and the issue of domain names have further complicated trademark laws. Nowhere is this more clear than online. The Internet, a breeding ground of originality, has given increase to many modern copyright controversies, not only infringements such as Napster and Grokster, but also less clear-cut and still unresolved issues such as Google Books or Viacom's suit against YouTube. Whatever the merits of the individual cases, it is becoming clearer all the time as the Internet's culture of innovation is running squarely into the brick wall of expansive copyright protection, extended online by the Digital Millennium Copyright Act.

Developments on the Internet are demonstrating by the minute that the balance has tipped too far in favor of the monopoly reward and too far away from encouraging innovation. As a consequence, there are, quite simply, many contexts in which copyright law is inept for the online and digital environment, dealing with great difficulty with derivative and transformative works.

Uniform Domain Name Dispute Resolution Policy (UDRP)

The UDRP requires that in each case the complainant must demonstrate that he has rights in a trademark. This has been, by all means, a remarkable event in the area of domain name disputes. Since that time, the processing and disposal of dispute has proceeded at a rate that is nothing short of astonishing. However, it was not supposed to be an ultimate remedy in each domain conflict.

Domain Name System

Choosing a domain name should be simple. You will want to make it unforgettable, pronounceable, concise, witty, simply spelled, and suggestive of the nature of the commerce on your Web site. However, even if your choice is exceptional from a marketing standpoint, it may not be as clever from a legal perspective. If you choose a domain name that clashes with any one of the millions of commercial names that already exist, you chance losing it. And if you have put money and effort into marketing your Web site and then are forced to give up the domain name, your Web-based business is likely to endure a damaging, if not mortal, blow. Customer confusion matters only if a domain name similar to the one you want to use is a protected trademark. To be protected, a trademark must be unique. A name may be distinguishing because it is made up, subjective in the context of its use, or evocative of the underlying product or service.

Choosing a domain name that pleases your own marketing needs and does not get in the way of another's trademark rights is possible. You should search as many accessible trademarks as possible, spot potential differences, and then pick a name that is unlikely to generate a letter from a displeased lawyer.

The first place to look is the trademark database of the U.S. Patent and Trademark Office at **www.uspto.gov.** Searching this database gives you all registered trademarks and all trademarks for which registration is pending. In the end, the responsibility belongs to the domain name registrant, as the trademark laws that apply in the hard copy world also apply on the Internet.

The Federal Trademark Dilution Act of 1995

The Federal Trademark Dilution Act of 1995 expanded the scope of rights granted to famous and distinctive trademarks under the Lanham Act. Dilution differs from normal trademark infringement in that there is no need to prove a likelihood of confusion to protect a mark. Instead, all that is required is that use of a "famous" mark by a third party causes the dilution of the "distinctive quality" of the mark.

Truth in Domain Names Act or Anti-Cyber-squatting Consumer Protection Act (ACCP)

The bill was enacted to protect consumers and promote electronic commerce by amending certain trademark infringement, dilution, and counterfeiting laws, and for other purposes. This act makes people registering domain names that are either trademarks or individual's names with the intent of selling the rights of the domain name to the trademark holder or individual for a profit liable to civil action. In order for a trademark owner to bring a claim under the ACCA, the owner should establish that: the trademark owner's mark is unique or famous, the domain name owner acted in bad faith to profit from the mark, and the domain name and the trademark are either impossible to tell apart or confusingly alike or dilutive for famous trademarks. The ACCA was passed to rectify what was perceived to be shortcomings with the current legal system. It was passed to protect consumers and American businesses, to promote the growth of online commerce, and to provide clarity in the law for trademark owners. It prohibits the bad faith and abusive registration of distinctive marks as Internet domain names with the intent to profit from the goodwill associated with such marks, a practice commonly referred to as "cyber squatting."

The Internet Corporation for Assigned Names and Numbers (ICANN)

ICANN is the non-profit corporation that was formed to assume responsibility for IP address allocation, protocol parameter assignment, domain name system management, and root server system management functions now performed under U.S. government contract by Internet Assigned Numbers Authority (IANA) and other entities. The tasks of ICANN include managing the assignment of domain names and IP addresses. To date, much of its work has concerned the introduction of new generic top-level domains. The technical work of ICANN is referred to as the IANA function; the rest of ICANN is mostly concerned with defining policy.

Chapter 13

The Trademark Process

"An image is not simply a trademark, a design, a slogan, or an easily remembered picture. It is a studiously crafted personality profile of an individual, institution, corporation, product, or service."

Daniel J. Boorstin

Trademarking your product names, business name, logos, slogans, and domain names is one of the most significant business decisions you will make. Trademark holders have the ability to prevent their competitors and other third parties from using their registered trademark without permission. A trademark is vital for all companies that profit from product name or business name recognition. Companies that fail to register their trademark, or companies presently conducting business using an unregistered trademark, run the risk of losing some or all of their rights for continued use. This usually happens when a competitor or unrelated third party trademarks a mark that is the same or considerably alike to an existing mark.

Registerability

To determine whether your mark appears to be registerable, use a trademark information form to provide a brief description of the goods or services that the mark will be utilized with, a brief description of the mark, and whether the mark is in actual use or is merely intended to be used in the future.

Distinctive Character

What makes a trademark distinctive in character? Trademark distinctiveness is a significant concept in the law governing trademarks and service marks. A trademark may be suitable for registration, or registerable, if among other things it executes the necessary trademark function and has distinctive character. Registerability can be understood as a continuum, with "inherently distinctive" marks at one end, "generic" and "descriptive" marks with no distinctive character at the other end, and "suggestive" and "arbitrary" marks lying between these two points. A mark must satisfy both sections to become registered.

State Laws

In order to obtain a trademark, all requirements must meet state and federal laws. One way to start is to check with the state you live in and begin the process there. To find out more information by state, visit **http://www.basicpatents.com/statelaw.htm**, which lists the laws and requirements each state has in order to obtain a trademark and patent.

Chapter 14

The Unprotected in Trademark Laws

"Project Xanadu is essentially my trademark. It was originally, and has returned to, my arms as that."

Ted Nelson

Trademark Protection

Trademarks are registered in classes for specific goods like perfume, soap, or automobiles. The scope of protection should be intently construed to the marketing area of the product. Conversely, with licensors licensing famous trademarks for an overabundance of products, that narrow scope of protection has stretched broadly in recent years.

Particular words or symbols cannot be appropriated as a trademark and may not be registered under the federal law known as the Lanham Act. These include: generic words (the common name of a thing, such as "piano," "concrete," "cigarette," "copy," or "car") and descriptive marks that merely describe a product or service which has not achieved recognition as functioning as a trademark (trademark practitioners call such recognition "secondary meaning," which is fully explained below). Descriptive marks may be registered on the supplemental register and then moved onto the principal register after secondary meaning is acquired. Geographically descriptive marks (i.e. the name of any state, city, or foreign nation are not protected either.)

You may register such a mark if it is not generally identifiable as a source of the goods or if you build secondary meaning over time through sales and advertising. Other items you may not register and which are not protected include: surnames (unless you build secondary meaning over time through sales and advertising); misleadingly descriptive marks; scandalous, immoral, or deceptive marks; disparaging words; marks suggesting a false connection with persons, institutions, beliefs, or national symbols; flags, coats of arms, or other U.S. insignia; an individual's name (without his or her consent); the name of a deceased U.S. president, while his widow is still alive; and trade names, unless used on goods or services in the same way a trademark is used.

In the United States, a trademark which has been registered with the USPTO uses the ® symbol. A business that does not actually register a trademark may instead use the common law designation "TM" in superscript next to the mark. Using the "TM" mark does not confer any legal rights in federal law, but it may help a business acquire secondary meaning for a mark.

Unlike copyright law, which provides for criminal penalties as well as civil damages, trademark law in the United States is entirely imposed through private lawsuits. The accountability is completely on the mark owner to file suit in either state or federal civil court in order to limit an infringing use. Failure to "police" a mark by stopping infringing uses can result in the loss of protection. Also, in contrast to copyright or patent law, trademark protection has no expiration. As long as the mark is repeatedly used, it can be indefinitely protected from infringement.

Chapter 15

Trademark Infringement

"The future of the nation depends in no small part on the efficiency of industry, and the efficiency of industry depends in no small part on the protection of intellectual property."

Judge Richard Posner

A variety of factors contribute to the extent of which a trademark owner may prevent unauthorized use of their trademarks.

What Constitutes Trademark Infringement?

If an organization owns the rights to a specific trademark, that organization can legally sue subsequent organizations for trademark infringement. The standard is "likelihood of confusion." To be more precise, the use of a trademark in connection with the sale of a good constitutes infringement if it is likely to cause consumer confusion as to the source of those goods or as to the sponsorship or approval of such goods. In deciding whether consumers are likely to be confused, the courts will typically look to a number of factors, including: the strength of the mark, the proximity of the goods, the similarity of the marks, evidence of actual confusion, the similarity of marketing channels used, the degree of caution exercised by the typical purchaser, and the defendant's intent.

Additionally, owners of trademarks can also bring an action for trademark dilution under either federal or state law. Beneath federal law, a dilution claim can be brought only if the mark is "famous." In deciding whether a mark is famous, the courts will look to the following factors: the degree of intrinsic or acquired uniqueness, the duration and extent of use, the total amount of advertising and publicity, the geographic extent of the market, the channels of trade, the degree of recognition in trading areas, any use of similar marks by third parties, or whether the mark is registered.

What happens if someone infringes on trademark laws?

There are many remedies for trademark infringement or dilution. Under federal law, successful plaintiffs are entitled to a wide range of remedies. Such plaintiffs are routinely awarded injunctions against further infringing or diluting use of the trademark. In trademark infringement suits, monetary relief may also be available, including: (1) defendant's profits, (2) damages sustained by the plaintiff, and (3) the costs of the action. Damages may be trebled upon showing bad faith. In trademark dilution suits, however, damages are available only if the defendant willfully traded on the plaintiff's goodwill in using the mark. Otherwise, plaintiffs in a dilution action are limited to injunctive relief.

Limits of Trademark Infringement

The reality is that few online trademark cases are taken to court. This is largely due to the costs associated with litigation and the usual willingness of both parties to settle amicably. The vast majority of trademark disputes are settled with either a friendly e-mail asking the infringing party to remove the material in question, or, failing that, a cease-and-desist letter (C&D). C&Ds can be expensive to have written, especially for a small business. In the real world, most businesses will have a draft C&D written and will customize it to each incident. Your lawyer will not like this approach, as it can result in some legal exposure, but that is the way it is usually done.

If a case is taken to court, you will want to have a federal registration for your trademark. This can be done online for about $30 at the U.S. Patent Office Web site. If you have federal registration, you can sue for up to three times the actual damages. Without it, you will be limited only to your damages. With trademarks, you have an obligation to defend them, or you limit your ability to enforce them. If a defendant can prove that you have been lax by not fighting every instance of trademark infringement, they can triumph against you. Your best defense is to produce documentation that shows you or your company has followed every instance of trademark infringement.

There are two types of infringement: trademark bidding and use of trademark within advertising copy. Trademark bidding is a "gray area" that has not yet been decided within the U.S. The Geico v. Google case is still not determined. That said, Google will not officially prevent competitors from bidding on your trademarks. Unofficially, there are many stories where they have done so. Despite this, you can always send a C&D to other companies who are bidding on your term. Frequently they will voluntarily remove the term from their campaign. Google and Yahoo will both stop advertisers from using your trademark terms within their advertising copy. You can file a complaint on a one-off basis (i.e. if there are certain companies which are allowed to use your trademarks or you can ask for a blanket restriction).

Chapter 16

Patents at a Glance

"To invent, you need a good imagination and a pile of junk."

Thomas Edison

Thomas Edison should know a little something about patents, as he held numerous in his lifetime. A patent is a set of exclusive rights granted by a state to an inventor or his assignee for a fixed period of time in exchange for a disclosure of an invention. It is a right granted for any device, substance, method, or process that is new, inventive, and useful. The modern-day patent originated in Europe, where the ruling nations awarded "letter patents" to a select few "favored" inventors. The United States enacted its first patent laws in 1790, as these laws were a part of the Constitution.

The term patent typically refers to a right granted to anyone who invents or discovers any new and functional process, machine, article of manufacture, arrangement of matter, or any new and useful enhancement thereof. In order for an invention to be eligible to be patented, it must be recent or new as defined in the patent law, which provides that an invention cannot be patented if: the invention was known or employed by others in this country, or patented or portrayed in a printed publication in this or a foreign country, before the invention thereof by the applicant for patent; or if the invention was patented or described in a printed publication in this or a foreign country or in public use or on sale in this country more than one year prior to the application for patent in the United States.

The patent laws of the United States were created and established to further the progress of science and what our forefathers deemed "useful arts." These initial laws granted limited time for authors and inventors to protect and profit from their works. It was not until Congress put into practice a series of laws protecting the first-to-patent structure that secured rights for the first to file for a patent. United States patent laws prohibit others from selling, making, using, offering for sale, or exporting the work of others who hold the patent for that product or service.

Patents are owned like real property. They can be sold, leased, or willed in an estate. Typically, manufacturers use the patent date or patent number as a selling feature. It implies their item is unique or incorporated a new idea. Most consumers were not aware that a design patent was only ornamental and would consider it the same as a utility patent. If anyone could copy or steal an invention, there would not be much incentive to establish new innovations, thus hurting the economy. Patents were intended to protect an invention for a set period of time to encourage the patent holder to invest time and money into the invention.

What is Patentable?

Under Title 35 of the United States Code, Section 101, who may obtain a patent is defined as follows: Whoever invents or discovers any new and useful process, machine, manufacture, or composition of matter, or any new and useful improvement thereof, may obtain a patent therefore, subject to the conditions and requirements of this title.

The following are what is patentable: any original, new, novel, or improved product or process in the subsequent main sections of technology; human necessities such as agriculture, food, personal, or domestic articles; health and amusement; performing operations such as separating, mixing, shaping, printing, and transporting; chemistry and metallurgy; textiles and paper; fixed construction such as building, earth–moving, mining, mechanical engineering, lighting, heating, weapons, blasting (including engines, pumps, and engineering in general); physics, such as instruments and nucleonic devices; and electricity.

There are exceptions. The following are not regarded as inventions and are excluded from patent protection: discoveries or findings that are products or processes of nature where mankind has not participated in their creation, including:

- Plants and microorganisms

- Business methods (i.e. credit or stock methods or computer programs)

- Scientific and mathematical methods and theories

- Schemes (i.e. investment, methods of bookkeeping, or insurance schemes)

- Rules for playing games where the game's equipment may be patentable

- Techniques for treatment of humans or animals by surgery or therapy, as well as diagnostic methods, except products,

(in particular substances or compositions or apparatus to employ in any of those methods)

- Public health-related manners of use or uses of any molecule or other substances at all used for the prevention or treatment of any disease which the user responsible for matters relating to health may assign as a serious health hazard or as a life-threatening disease

- Simple presentation of information, and non-functional particulars of shape, configuration, pattern, or ornamentation

Copyright and patent laws grant the inventors the exclusive right to the invention. These laws prohibit the reproduction of the invention for a set period of time and are intended to protect the inventors.

The United States Patent and Trademark Offices asserts, "If the invention has been described in a printed publication anywhere in the world, or if it was known or used by others in this country before the date that the applicant made his/her invention, a patent cannot be obtained. If the invention has been described in a printed publication anywhere, or has been in public use or on sale in this country more than one year before the date on which an application for patent is filed in this country, a patent cannot be obtained."

As author James L. Rogers notes in his book, *Protect Your Patent*, "Thousands of patents are issued to inventors each year." So try it! No matter who you are, people like you secure patents every year. Obtaining a patent is a cause for a special celebration, and you have taken the first step in making sure your ideas are safe by purchasing this book.

A patent for an invention is the grant of a property right to the inventor, issued by the United States Patent and Trademark Office. Generally, the term of a new patent is 20 years from the date on which the application for the patent was filed in the United States or, in special cases, from the date an earlier related application was filed, subject to the payment of maintenance fees. U.S. patent grants are effective only within the United States, U.S. territories, and U.S. possessions.

In his article "Protect Your Ideas with Copyrights and Patents," Tim Knox says, "A wise man once said, 'The biggest difference between a copyright and a patent is the number of lawyers it takes to do the paperwork.'" In reality, most patent owners make arrangements with existing companies to sell their inventions. One, the financial responsibilities are colossal, and two, a larger company has a more realistic chance of making the invention a commercial success. This arrangement is done through a license agreement, in which the licensee is sanctioned to commercially market and distribute the invention, and in exchange the patent owner collects royalties for each invention sold.

Rogers also notes "to maximize the protection and utilization of your patented invention, you should consider various forms of intellectual property protection in addition to relying on the rights provided by your patent." You can patent your idea and can trademark it to differentiate it from other products sold under the range of your patent. A domain name can support your business of promoting your patent, confidential agreements can thwart the loss of your patent rights altogether, and trade secrets safeguard the knowledge used in developing your patented invention.

Getting a patent will not be easy, but nothing worthwhile is. Why is it so hard to obtain a patent? In order for your invention to earn a patent, there are rigorous examination procedures conducted by the USPTO. This is to ensure that your idea or invention is original and not just a novelty. One of the best ways to ensure that your patent is free of potential dangers which trap other patents is to, as Rogers states, "Keep your patent in force by paying all necessary maintenance fees when they become due and by making sure that competitors will not somehow sneak around the coverage of your claimed invention."

Maintenance fees, you will learn after submitting your invention to the USPTO, will cost you. The USPTO charges fees for just about everything you submit to them. The USPTO also charges fees even after you receive your patent. Initially the only thing you must worry about submitting to the USPTO is the fee itself. These fees absolutely must be paid if you wish your patent to remain in force.

Where and how do you pay those fees? The easiest and simplest way is to pay the USPTO online at their Web site, **www.uspto. gov**. What happens if you err and miss a maintenance fee? You will have to petition the USPTO and explain why your delay in payment was either unavoidable or unintentional. In order to gain this petition, you must provide specific details and facts, which indicate how you took the steps to pay the maintenance fees, but through circumstances beyond your control you could not pay the fees at the time of the application.

Patent law consists of three types: utility, design, and plant. The most widespread form is utility. These are granted to the creator or inventor of a new, non-palpable invention.

Utility patents may be granted to anyone who invents or comes across any new and helpful process, machine, article of manufacture, or composition of matter, or any new and useful enhancement thereof. This additional qualification is used in countries such as the United States to differentiate them from additional sorts of patents, although this should not be confused with utility models granted by other countries.

Examples of specific species of patents for inventions incorporate biological patents, business method patents, chemical patents, and software patents. Other types of intellectual property rights are referred to as patents in some jurisdictions. Industrial design rights are called design patents in some jurisdictions, as they protect the visual design of objects that are not merely utilitarian. Design patents may be granted to anyone who invents a new, unique, and decorative design for an article of manufacture.

Plant breeders' rights are sometimes called plant patents. Plant patents may be granted to anyone who creates or discovers and asexually replicates any distinct and new category of plant. Patents cannot and will not be granted for artistic creations, mathematical models, plans, schemes, or other purely mental processes.

Before you apply, consider this: The issue of patenting should be considered an integral part of your overall business strategy. It is as important as finance, production, marketing, and profit potential. Filing a provisional application can be quite inexpensive and affords you 12 months to consider alternatives if your patent is rejected.You will be in a better position to decide if further expense and effort will be required in the patenting process.

There have been instances when multiple applications have been filed for the same invention. If you discover this, it will be up to an official patent examiner to declare that an interference exists between the two or more applications. A hearing is then held to determine the fate of the ownership of the patent or who is entitled to the award of the patent. This is very much like a judicial proceeding. Affidavits and declarations are submitted and reviewed, and sometimes even live testimony is heard. In the end, whoever receives the patent relies on certain variables such as who first conceived the invention, who was the first to build and test the invention, and who was the first to file a provisional or regular patent application.

There are alternatives for protection. You can file an international application, which allows you to defer the costs of obtaining patents overseas, while you decide which foreign markets should be protected. Or you may trademark it using a word or symbol that distinguishes your invention, product, or service.

Anyone can file for a patent and even be granted one. The actor Marlon Brando dabbled with some innovations in his last years. Brando had several patents issued in his name from the U.S. Patent and Trademark Office, all of which are directed to a drumhead-tensioning device and method between June 2002 and November 2004. For an example, see U.S. Patent 6,812,392 and its equivalents.

What About Internationally Filing for a Patent?

There is no such entity as a true international patent. The majority of the foremost industrial countries of the world are members of the Patent Cooperation Treaty (PCT), which is overseen by the World Intellectual Property Organization (WIPO).

It is vital to note that patents are territorial rights. A patent granted in South Africa can be enforced in South Africa only.

Nevertheless, you may, within 12 months of filing your South African provisional patent application, file foreign patent applications based on your provisional patent application. You will only have an enforceable patent right in these countries once each foreign patent application has proceeded to grant. This does not mean you cannot start marketing your invention in these countries; it means that you cannot obtain a patent right if you do not file and prosecute each patent to completion in each of your target markets. Thus, there is no such thing as a "worldwide" patent — you have to file a patent application in each country in which you wish to protect your invention.

You do not have to be a qualified genius to hold a patent. You must, however, have an original idea or improvement to an existing idea in order to qualify.

For an example of a patent, please refer to the patent issued to Marlon Brando at the end of this book. Please notice all the detail that goes into the descriptions of the invention. Marlon Brando was more than an actor; he was also an inventor and perhaps, like you, a patent owner.

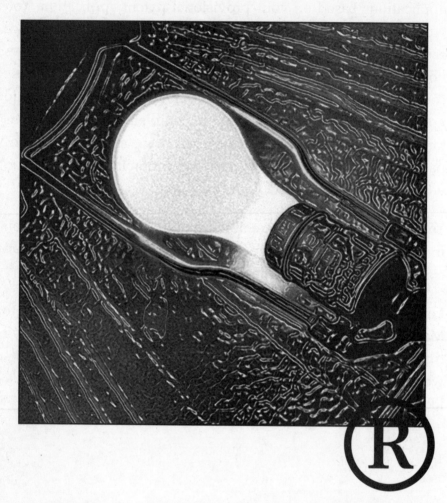

Thomas Edison patented the
lightbulb on Jan. 27, 1880.

Chapter 17

Legislation of Patents

".... the fairness of the patent laws is contested on the ground that they reward only those who put the finishing touch leading to practical utilization of achievements on many predecessors. These precursors go empty-handed although their contribution to the final result was often much more weighty than that of the patentee."

L. Mises, Human Action: A Treatise of Economics, 1949

President George Washington signed the first Patent Act in 1790. Prior to this, some patents were issued by individual states. The first patent in the United States granted under the 1790 Patent Act was issued to Samuel Hopkins of Philadelphia, Pennsylvania on July 31, 1790. This was patent X1 and was for a new process in making potash and pearl ash. Prior to July 13, 1836, patents were not given numbers at the time of issue. The issue date and the inventor identified them. In 1836, a fire destroyed the U. S. Patent Offices, and all the records for these early patents were destroyed. It is estimated that there had been just fewer than 10,000 patents issued before the fire. The records for these early patents were recreated when possible and were then given a number with an X. The highest X patent number in the U. S. Patent Office database is X9900. On July 13, 1836, the numbering sequence started over again with the number 1.

Patent law identifies the rules for patents. The USPTO oversees all patent laws concerning the granting of patents and numerous other provisions relating to patents. They will scrutinize your applications and grant patents when applicants are entitled to them. They publish and distribute all patent information, including: recording assignments of patents, maintaining search files of U.S. and foreign patents, preserving a search room for public use in examining distributed patents and records, and providing copies of patents and official records to the public.

First Patent Act: April 7, 1790

The Patent Act of 1790 was the United States' first patent statute. It was titled "An Act" to promote the progress of useful arts and passed on April 10, 1790, after being submitted on the 7th of April. It granted the applicant the "sole and exclusive right and liberty of making, constructing, using, and vending to others to be used" of his invention, for a period of 14 years.

Title 35 of the United States Code

This states that a person shall be entitled to a patent unless the invention was known or used by others in this country, or patented or described in a printed publication in this or a foreign country, before the invention thereof by the applicant for patent, or the invention was patented or described in a printed publication in this or a foreign country or in public use or on sale in this country, more than one year prior to the date of the application for patent in the United States, or has abandoned the invention, or the invention was first patented or caused to be patented, or was the subject of an inventor's certificate, by the applicant or his legal representatives or assigns in a foreign country prior to the date of the application for patent in this country on an application for patent or inventor's certificate filed more than 12 months before the filing of the application in the United States.

Or the invention was described in (1) an application for patent, published under section 122(b) [35 USC 122(b)], by another filed in the United States before the invention by the applicant for patent, or (2) a patent granted on an application for patent by another filed in the United States before the invention by the applicant for patent, except that an international application filed under the treaty defined in section 351(a) [35 USC 351(a)] shall have the effects for the purposes of this subsection of an application filed in the United States only if the international application designated the United States and was published under Article 21(2) of such treaty in the English language; or he did not himself invent the subject matter sought to be patented, or during the course of an interference conducted under section 135 [35 USC 135] or section 291 [35 USC 291], another inventor involved therein establishes, to the extent permitted in section 104 [35 USC 104], that before such person's invention thereof the invention was made by such other inventor and not abandoned, suppressed, or concealed.

Or before such person's invention thereof, another inventor who had not abandoned, suppressed, or concealed it made the invention in this country. In determining priority of invention under this subsection, there shall be considered not only the respective dates of conception and reduction to practice of the invention, but also the reasonable diligence of one who was first to conceive and last to reduce to practice, from a time prior to conception by the other.

The Patent Act of 1836

The Patent Act of 1836 established a number of important changes in the U.S. patent system, including the examination of patent applications prior to issuing a patent. This was the first time this was done anywhere in the world. Prior to this, patents were issued on all applications, even of they were direct copies of earlier patents. It was left to the courts to decide validity in the event of a lawsuit. Another change was the hiring of professional patent examiners. Initially only one examiner was hired, but soon a second one was hired to handle the increased workload. A library of prior art was also established to assist in examinations.

Plant Patent Act of 1930

The Plant Patent Act of 1930 is a U.S. federal law spurred by the work of Luther Burbank. This piece of legislation made it possible to patent new varieties of plants, excluding sexual and tuber-propagated plants. Thomas Edison testified before Congress in support of the legislation.

Invention Secrecy Act of 1951

The Invention Secrecy Act of 1951 is a body of U.S. federal law intended to prevent discovery of new inventions and technologies that, in the opinion of selected U.S. agencies, demonstrate a possible threat to the national security of the United States. The government has long wanted to control the issue of new technologies that might threaten the national defense and economic stability of the country. During World War I, Congress authorized the USPTO to classify particular defense-related patents. This original effort lasted only for the length of that war but was re-employed in

October 1941 in expectation of the U.S. entry into World War II. Patent secrecy orders were initially planned to remain effective for two years, beginning on July 1, 1940, but were later extended for the duration of the war. The Invention Secrecy Act of 1951 made such patent secrecy permanent.

American Inventors Protection Act (AIPA)

The American Inventors Protection Act (AIPA) is a U.S. federal law enacted on November 29, 1999 as Public Law 106-113. In 2002, the Intellectual Property and High Technology Technical Amendments Act of 2002, Public Law 107-273, amended AIPA. The basic scenario of this act is that a patent applicant allows its application to languish in the USPTO while watching another company make substantial investments in a technology or product that will infringe the yet-to-be-issued patent. Once the other company's sunk costs are large, the patent applicant obtains the patent, asserts infringement, and "holds up" the other company, demanding supra-competitive royalties for a license to the "submarine patent." The company must agree to supra-competitive royalties or forego its production or innovation. As a result, consumers will either pay higher prices for the company's goods, or will never get the benefit of the innovation that the company had to abandon.

Bayh-Dole Act

The Bayh-Dole Act, or University and Small Business Patent Procedures Act, is a piece of U.S. legislation from 1980. Among other things, it gave U.S. universities, small businesses, and non-profits intellectual property control of their inventions that resulted from federal government-funded research, allowing them to elect to engage in ownership of an invention before the government. The act was sponsored by two senators, Birch Bayh of Indiana and Bob Dole of Kansas, and was enacted by the United States Congress on December 12, 1980. The Bayh-Dole Act is a significant 20th century piece of legislation in the field of intellectual property in the U.S.

Patent Reform Act of 2005 (did not pass)

Texas Republican Congressman Lamar S. Smith introduced the Act on June 8, 2005. This act would have harmonized American patent law with the patent laws of the rest of the world, changing U.S. patent law from first-to-invent to first–to-file. Even under a first-to-invent system, the first-inventor-in-fact does not always obtain entitlement to a patent. It also was intended to expand the use of post-issuance re-examination and opposition proceedings, as well as limit access to injunctions along with some modifications to other patent legislation.

Patent Reform Act of 2007

In the Patent Reform Act of 2007, Democratic Congressman Howard Berman introduced the House of Representatives bill on April 18, 2007. Democratic Party Senator Patrick Leahy introduced the Senate bill that same day. The bills generally resemble the proposed Patent Reform Act of 2005, which would have enacted many of the proposals recommended by a 2003 report by the Federal Trade Commission and a 2004 report by the National Academy of Sciences. The United States is presently the only country in the world that gives priority to the application, which claims the earliest invention date, regardless of which application arrives first. The first-to-invent system is thought to benefit small inventors, who may be less experienced with the patent application system and procedures.

The European Patent Convention (EPC)

The European Patent Convention (EPC) created the European Patent Office (EPO), which is based in Germany. The convention currently applies to most European Economic Community member states and to several other European countries. The EPC provides for a single application in English, German, or French, on which a central search and examination is carried out. Once the patent is accepted for grant and the appropriate fees and translations are submitted, the single application is converted into a bundle of individual national patents. The system also allows an opposition to the grant to be lodged at the EPO within nine months from patent grant. Subsequent issues of validity, however, must be dealt with on a country-by-country basis by individual national courts.

Patent Cooperation Treaty (PCT)

This system, which includes many countries in addition to European countries, similarly provides for the filing of a single application designating the member countries from which patents are desired. Although the single filing takes place under the auspices of the World Intellectual Property Organization (WIPO), a specialized agency of the United Nations system that seeks to promote international cooperation in the protection of international property, the actual filing is made either in the United States or the EPO. The single application is searched, and it is possible to request a nonbinding opinion on patentability. After the payment of the appropriate fees and the filing of appropriate translations, the application is converted into a bundle of individual national applications, which are then subject to examination by individual national patent offices.

North American Free Trade Agreement (NAFTA)

The North American Free Trade Agreement (NAFTA) is a general trade agreement between Canada, Mexico, and the U.S. that imposes general requirements for both the domestic and international treatment and enforcement of intellectual property rights.

NAFTA significantly advances protection of intellectual property in Mexico. However, it also requires that the United States and Canada make certain changes. The agreement recognizes the need, at a minimum, to accede and give effect to the main international conventions relating to intellectual property, including the Paris Convention (intellectual property), the Berne Convention (copyrights), the Geneva Convention (protects phonograms or audio works), and the Union for the Protection of New Varieties of Plants (UPOV).

Under the UPOV, protection is given to plant varieties that:

- belong to one of the botanical species on the national list

- are distinct from commonly known varieties

- are sufficiently homogeneous

- are stable

In essence, NAFTA requires each member country to extend

protection to foreign nationals equivalent to the protection granted to domestic rights holders.

Intellectual Property Protection Restoration Act of 2003 (Introduced in the Senate)

The purposes of this act are to help eliminate the unfair commercial advantage that states and their instrumentalities now hold in the federal intellectual property system because of their ability to obtain protection under the U.S. patent, copyright, and trademark laws while remaining exempt from liability for infringing the rights of others; promote technological innovation and artistic creation in furtherance of the policies underlying federal laws and international treaties relating to intellectual property; reaffirm the availability of prospective relief against state officials who are violating or who threaten to violate federal intellectual property laws; and abrogate state sovereign immunity in cases where states or their instrumentalities, officers, or employees violate the United States Constitution by infringing federal intellectual property.

U.S. Patent and Trademark Modernization Act of 2003

As introduced in the Senate

Amends federal patent law to: lower patent filing and basic national fees; increase excess claims, disclaimer, appeal, extension, revival, and maintenance fees; and add new application examination, patent search, and patent issuance fees.

Engrossed as agreed to or passed by the House

Amends federal patent law to reduce the filing fee for an application for: an original patent from $690 to $300; an original design patent from $310 to $200; a plant patent from $480 to $200; and reissue of a patent from $690 to $300. Changes from $670, $690, $970, and $96, in different specified circumstances to $300 for the basic national fee for each international application filed under the Patent Cooperation Treaty done at Washington, on June 19, 1970, entering the national stage. Increases from $150 to $200 the patent filing fee for a provisional application for an original patent.

The Internet and Patents

The Internet and a "liberalized" software patent practice are creating a boom in the U.S. software industry. The industry has been growing at an average of 20 percent over the past few years and will continue to grow for some time. This is due to the fact that software is often pirated from larger companies and copied, then handed out to employees in smaller companies to cut the cost of buying large amounts of software. This is illegal, and the government has teamed with software industry giants to try to prevent this from continuing. Copyright protection for software is currently undergoing a rebuilding phase. The courts apply the prohibition in Statute 17 of the U.S.C. under Section 102 (b) against copyrighting piracy. Yet there is still a tremendous amount of confusion in the software industry in regard to the patenting of software. Technically, it is virtually impossible to patent a computer program because disks are easily copied. It is generally believed that software is unpatentable.

The Stevenson-Wydler Act

The Stevenson-Wydler Act establishes various administrative structures to encourage commercialization and specifies that if the research institution claims ownership and fails to commercialize, then the employee inventor can obtain title (subject to the government obtaining a non-exclusive license).

Mary Dixon Kies was the first woman ever awarded a patent. In 1809 she patented a process of weaving straw with silk or thread. This process boosted the economy and helped the hat industry.

Chapter 18

Types of Patents

"Technology moves now with a speed once undreamed of — its swift march dictates a shortening of the life of a patent."

W. Hamilton, Patents and Free Enterprise, Temporary [U. S.]
National Economic Committee, 1941

Now we will cover the types of patents with information and descriptions, as well as an introduction to which type of patent you need for what you are registering for.

Biological Patents

This is a patent relating to an invention or discovery in biology. The 1970s marked the first time scientists patented methods on their biotechnological inventions with recombinant DNA. It was not until 1980 that patents for whole-scale living organisms were allowed. In Diamond v. Chakrabarty, the Supreme Court overturned a previous precedent allowing the patentability of living matter. The subject for this specific case was a bacterium that was purposely modified to help clean up and degrade oil spills.

Legal changes began in 1980. Since then, there has been a universal trend of patenting inventions on living matter. Biotech and pharmaceutical companies in recent years have found out how profitable biological research can be. These firms promote many research opportunities by funding made possible only through the private sector.

Business Method Patent

These are a class of patents, which reveal and assert new methods of doing business. This includes new kinds of e-commerce, insurance, banking, and tax compliance. Business method patents are a fairly new species of patent, and there have been several reviews investigating the suitability of patenting business methods.

Chemical Patent

This is an important source of technical and bibliographic information. Chemical patents are different from other sources of technical information because of the generic Markush structures contained within them, named after the inventor Eugene Markush, who won a claim in the U.S. in 1925 to allow such structures to be used in patent claims. These generic structures are used to make the patent claim as broad as possible. Chemical patents are particularly important in the pharmaceuticals industry, where they are used to protect the large investments necessary to develop drugs.

Software Patent

Software patent does not have a generally accepted definition. One definition suggested by the Foundation for a Free Information

Infrastructure is that a software patent is a "patent on any performance of a computer realized by means of a computer program." Utility patents are now available to cover virtually any form or type of software-related inventions. Among the protected forms are:

- Application programs (such as spreadsheet programs and databases

- Operating systems

- Web browsers

- User interfaces

- Software for implementing business systems

- Data structures

- Utility programs

- Data compression

- Virus detection

- Programming languages

- Software on a computer disk

- Software in a computer memory

- Software in digital form carried on a transmission media

Mathematical Algorithms

Patents are accessible to guard mathematical algorithms or

formulas that are "applied" to a problem having an association with the physical world, such as the dispensation of data representative of real world objects. It is difficult and often complicated to determine whether an algorithm is properly "applied" to allow it to be part of a patented invention . A couple of examples may be of assistance for when an algorithm is applied. A mathematical algorithm used in a data compression process, for example, is "applied" because data compression is a established statutory type of process. Nonetheless, using a mathematical algorithm in accounting software will not be correctly applied if it simply calculates a new balance or other number, which does not control the flow of the software.

Plant Patents

On the word of the USPTO, "The law also provides for the granting of a patent to anyone who has invented or discovered and asexually reproduced any distinct and new variety of plant, including cultivated sports, mutants, hybrids, and newly found seedlings, other than a tuber-propagated plant or a plant found in an uncultivated state. Asexually propagated plants are those that are reproduced by means other than from seeds, such as by the rooting of cuttings, by layering, budding, grafting, inarching, etc."

Design Patents

In the United States, a design patent is a patent granted on the ornamental design of a functional item. Design patents are a type of industrial design right. Ornamental designs of jewelry, furniture, beverage containers, and computer icons are examples of what can be covered by design patents.

Utility Model

A utility model is a constitutional domination arranged for a limited time in exchange for an inventor providing enough teaching of his or her invention to allow a person of normal skill in the pertinent art to perform the invention.

Genetic Patents

Genetic patents are patents on specific genetic sequences, their usage, and often their chemical composition. There is controversy over whether these patents advance technology by providing scientists with an incentive to create, or hinder research by creating bureaucratic red tape and fees to utilize research that is patented.

Landmarks in the History of Genetic Patents

In 1998, developmental biologist Stuart Newman applied for a patent on a process to produce a "chimerical" creature. Newman had no intention of actually making the part-human, part-animal monster — he just wanted to spark public debate.

But in 1999, the USPTO rejected his application. Newman announced his attention to appeal, if necessary all the way up to the Supreme Court.

In 2005, he lost his seven-year battle when the USPTO once more rejected the claim, saying the hybrid would be too closely related to a human to be patentable.

Samuel Hopkins received the first patent issued July 30, 1790. He invented a new process for making potash, an ingredient used in fertilizer.

Chapter 19

Patent Eligibility (Patentability)

"In the field of industrial patents in particular we shall have seriously to examine whether the award of a monopoly privilege is really the most appropriate and effective form of reward for the kind of risk bearing which investment in scientific research involves."

F. Hayek, Individualism and Economic Order, 1948

A patent is a grant of a property right, which permits an inventor to exclude others from making, using, or selling the invention disclosed and claimed in the patent.

When you get a great idea, make sure 1) your patent search documents your idea to serve as a record of invention date and, 2) do not waste time developing an idea that already exists.

Each type of patent confers the right to exclude others from infringing on the invention, industrial design, or plant variety. Patents do not protect ideas, but rather structures and methods that apply technological concepts. In return for getting a patent and receiving the right to exclude others, the inventor must relinquish the secrecy of the invention and fully disclose the best mode of making and using the invention to the public.

Requirements for Patent Applications

If you want your idea to be patented, you need to meet three legal requirements:

1. **Novelty** — The technology is not "anticipated" or identical to an invention disclosed in a single piece of prior art.

2. **Non-obviousness** — The technology must be different enough from the prior art not to be obvious.

3. **Utility** — The invention must have a useful purpose. Virtually all inventions meet the utility requirement, which has largely been used to prevent the patenting of "quack" inventions such as perpetual motion machines.

Who May Apply for a Patent?

According to U.S. law, only the inventor may apply for a patent. If the inventor is deceased, the inventor's legal representatives. For example, the administrator or executor of the estate may make application. If the inventor is mentally incapacitated, a guardian may make the application for a patent.

Standards for Patentability

In general, the provisions of 35 U.S.C. § 102 necessitate an invention be original as compared to prior technology. The provisions of 35 U.S.C. § 103 require an invention to be "non-obvious," as associated to prior technology. Key requirements of § 102 and § 103 can be summarized as follows. To obtain a patent, the applicant(s) must be the inventor(s) (i.e. they must have originated the invention, not copied (derived) it); the invention must be novel — that is, it must be diverse from prior art inventions; the invention cannot be "obvious" to one of ordinary skill in the art to which the invention pertains; prior art usually includes all technology publicly known prior to the invention, and all technology known after the invention if it was disclosed in a publication, presented for sale or publicly used for more than a year before the filing date of the patent application on the invention; and "non-obviousness" is subjective, but can be established by looking at the following features: the invention answers a long-felt need and attains unanticipated results, benefits from commercial success, or suggests surprise in the trade.

CASE STUDY: APPLYING PATENTS TO INTERNET MUSIC TECHNOLOGY

Imagine a group of computer programmers who had been laid off by the National Security Agency due to the end of the Cold War. The group calls itself Music-Org and plans on starting a music publishing business on the Internet. The founders are all frustrated amateur musicians who were unable to make it as professional musicians. They are all convinced that, had they been able to publish their music, they would have been "discovered" and become multi-millionaire musicians. They now believe it is too late to make it in music, but that there is money to be made on the Internet publishing music.

Music-Org plans to acquire a surplus Dale supercomputer and use it to establish a Web site they will use to custom-publish musical recordings. For a fee, Music-Org will take a recording from an aspiring musician and make it available over the Internet. Music-Org's home page will include a directory of all available musicians and their titles. A customer will order a recording by selecting it from a directory and supplying Music-Org with a credit card number and an authorization.

Music-Org will then download the recording to the customer over the Internet, and the customer will save the recording to their hard drive. To get the data quickly over the Internet, Music-Org has invented a super-compression algorithm that can reduce an hour's worth of recorded music to 40 kilobytes of data and encrypt it.

CASE STUDY: APPLYING PATENTS TO INTERNET MUSIC TECHNOLOGY

Music-Org will also provide a small computer program, or applet, which will run on a customer's computer to decompress, decrypt, and play the recording to the computer's speaker system.

In addition, Music-Org plans on using the Dale supercomputer to automatically synthesize a music video for each recording, using a photograph of the recording musician. The recording musician will be able to direct the synthesizing of the video by working interactively with the Dale supercomputer over the Internet. These music videos will also be downloaded with the accompanying music and be playable by the applet along with the recording.

To advertise their services, Music-Org intends to monitor Internet data traffic on the Web and identify potential customers by, for instance, looking at who subscribes to music-oriented bulletin boards and Web sites. Music-Org intends to e-mail potential customers sales literature for their Web site. To do this, Music-Org has invented a Web-Spy that can secretly monitor any Web site and capture the names and e-mail addresses of visitors.

Music-Org's home page system also is capable of presenting a customized home page to each visitor-customer to the site, based on information Music-Org has acquired about the visitor. This way, the visitor-customer is first presented with the sales literature and recordings they are most likely to want to buy, to save time for them and the Web site. Music-Org has developed a program, which can predict with 97% accuracy which titles a visitor-customer will want to buy.

Not to be outclassed by whatever competition they might encounter, Music-Org plans to pay a Madison Avenue graphic artist and a user-interface specialist $200,000 to design the most artistically aesthetic and functional home page on the Internet. The new design will combine superior ease-of-use features with striking graphic images.

By the way, Music-Org has already had a public offering and raised $50 million. All of the founders are already millionaires on paper, and they have not even bought the Dale supercomputer yet.

PATENT ADVICE FOR MUSIC-ORG

Music-Org is the perfect example of a client that will benefit from aggressive patent protection for their Internet business.

CASE STUDY: APPLYING PATENTS TO INTERNET MUSIC TECHNOLOGY

A patent attorney would ask Music-Org's members when they developed their ideas and if they have been used, published, or offered for sale. Next, the attorney would docket a deadline for filing U.S. applications and advise them not to disclose or sell a system prior to the filing date of their U.S. patent application(s) to preserve foreign filing rights.

Next, the question is: what would Music-Org really like to patent to protect its core business? They say the core of their business is the fee-for-service publishing of recordings. They are then advised to file a patent claiming an invention, which is comprised of a database containing:

- Recordings

- Data specifying an owner of each recording

- Data specifying the number of times each recording is sold to a customer over the Internet

- Software for receiving orders for a recording at a home page and for electronically transferring the ordered recording over the Internet to a customer software for reading the database and reporting to each owner the number of times their recording has been sold in a period of time

The USPTO will likely find that this claim meets the novelty requirement of 35 U.S.C. Section 102, assuming Music-Org is indeed the first company to devise this invention. However, an examiner might find this particular invention obvious and do his or her best to refuse the patent coverage.

Since there seem to be other good prospects for patent coverage in their business concept, one of the most promising is the idea of synthesizing music videos and distributing them with the recording. The elements of the invention might look like:

- A database containing:

- recordings

- a synthesized music video for each recording

- software for receiving orders for a recording at a home page and for electronically transferring the ordered recording and its music video over the Internet to a customer

CASE STUDY: APPLYING PATENTS TO INTERNET MUSIC TECHNOLOGY

Music-Org could also add to this invention the step of transferring to the customer an applet that the customer uses to play the video and record on the customer's PC.

Music-Org should also be advised to patent their compression/encryption algorithm software but not limit their coverage solely to music and video data compression.

An additional patent or patents could be obtained on Music-Org's system for synthesizing music videos.

Music-Org can also look at patenting its Web-Spy. Additionally, Music-Org may want to patent its sales-prediction software, and the application of that software to control the presentation of materials to a visitor-customer of a home page on the Internet.

Music-Org must consider patenting the new user-interface they are having developed: the functionality of the interface with a utility patent, and the aesthetics/ornamentation with a series of design patents.

Music-Org is also advised to patent the data structure of its encrypted recording/video files, as stored on a storage media such as a floppy disk, a hard disk, a computer memory, or in electromagnetic form traveling over a copper cable or optical fiber from one computer to another. Music-Org should also protect its applet in computer-code form, as stored on a recording media or transported in digital electromagnetic form.

Music-Org uses a variety of combinations of the above-noted concepts and inventions, and that they should consider seeking protection for as many different combinations as are commercially valuable.

ADVISING MUSIC-ORG ON INFRINGEMENT ISSUES

There are a few infringement issues that Music-Org should consider. First, United Corporation has a patent on data compression called the LZW data compression algorithm. Music-Org's compression algorithm might infringe this patent.

A company called Interactive Gift Express, Inc., claims to have a patent on reproducing information in material objects in a point of sale location.

Additionally, there was once a patent issued claiming to cover the placement of advertising inside of a computer program to be displayed to a user of the program.

CASE STUDY: APPLYING PATENTS TO INTERNET MUSIC TECHNOLOGY

This patent has been rejected by the USPTO in a re-examination proceeding, but might issue after amendment and argument by the applicant Music-Org to avoid putting advertising in their applet downloaded to customers.

CONCLUSION

The Internet will provide many interesting business opportunities. Being an inherently electronic marketplace, patent protection should be carefully considered, particularly in view of the recent liberalization of software patent practice.

Garrett Morgan received a patent in 1923 for a 3-way traffic signal. He found stop and go signals dangerous because they had no buffer to slow traffic.

Chapter 20

Patent Ownership & Rights

"Except, perhaps, cases of warranty of horses, there was no subject which offered so many opportunities for sharp practice as the law of patents."

Earl of Granville, Parliamentary Debates, House of Lords, 1851

Under United States common law, an individual owns rights in any invention they generate, in spite of whether that invention was fashioned in the course of employment. In the absence of a clear common law right to inventions created by academics, most universities have ratified intellectual property policies, which assert to claim ownership of inventions made using university resources and/or in the sequence of employment.

One of the most noteworthy features of the United States framework is the existence of federal legislation (the Bayh-Dole Act) governing inventions produced with project-specific public funds. Under the Bayh-Dole Act, universities and government funding agencies enter into a funding contract, which grants a right of ownership to the university subject to a number of responsibilities. Most significantly, the university must obey a variety of obligations concerning disclosure of the invention, select whether to retain title, royalty sharing, and preference to small businesses and U.S. industry.

If the university does not meet the terms of the above obligations or opts not to take title, the Bayh-Dole Act put into practice regulations for the government to receive title by giving written notice. The inventor can apply to the government for title. If the university fulfills its obligations, it will be allowed to keep title and commercialize the invention. The government will still have clear, minimum rights, including a non-exclusive binding license to use the invention throughout the world. The government will also have "march-in rights," which permit it to make the university grant a license to a third party where the university does not succeed to commercialize the invention, where licensing is necessary for health and safety needs, or where preference for U.S. industry has not been observed.

Invention ownership in government research organizations is ruled exclusively by national technology transfer legislation. The United States government can assert ownership of inventions created by public servants under the authority of Executive Order No 10096 and its implementing regulations, except if the government's contribution is not adequate to justify the assignment of ownership. Once a government research institution claims ownership of an invention, that organization will be grateful under the Stevenson-Wydler Act to commercialize it where suitable.

Profiles of Famous Inventors

Stanley Mason

Inventor of everyday products

Stanley Mason has more than 55 U.S. patents and is responsible for inventing products we use every day. His inventions include the squeezable ketchup bottle, stringless Band-Aid packaging, dental floss dispensers, instant splints and casts for broken limbs, the first granola bars, fingerprinting systems, heated pizza boxes, heat-proof microwave cookware, masonware, countless toys and games, and the world's first form-fitted disposable diaper with sticky tabs rather than pins. Mason sold his first invention at the age of 7.

Dr. Percy Spencer

Owner of the microwave patent

Did you know that a melted candy bar changed the way we heat foods? Dr. Percy Spencer was self-taught and learned what he learned from his unlimited curiosity. Later in his life, Dr. Spencer was working at Raytheon testing a new vacuum tube called a magnetron. He was standing in front of it when he discovered that the candy bar in his pocket had melted. And then he did what inventors do — he tested some another object! He placed some popcorn kernels near the tube and watched as the popcorn sputtered, cracked, and popped all over his lab. Next, he cooked an egg. Finally, he built the first microwave oven, which later became a fixture in almost every kitchen.

Hedy Lamarr

Creator of various inventions

Actress and inventor Hedy Lamarr's life story is far more fascinating than any of her movies. She was known as one of the most gorgeous women to ever appear in films, as well as a Hollywood social butterfly. At a party, she met composer George

Antheil and was sitting on his piano when the concept for the torpedo guidance system came to her. Her frequency-hopping idea is the basis for modern communication technology in devices ranging from cordless telephones to WiFi Internet connections. Lamarr was not just an actress — she was a great inventor.

Beulah Henry

Creator of various inventions

Beulah Henry was called "the lady Edison" because of her unyielding pursuit of inventive thinking. In 1912, at the age of 25, she developed her first of more than 100-patented inventions — a vacuum ice cream freezer. Ms. Henry also made improvements to typewriters that were merely early concepts of duplicating written documents, and bobbin-free sewing machines. She invented for herself and for companies who hired her to make improvements to their existing products. She was exceptionally smart and very wealthy, as she founded a number of manufacturing companies to create her inventions.

Lonnie Johnson

Patent holder of the Supersoaker and other inventions, Lonnie Johnson is a well-known African-American who invented the world-famous water gun the Supersoaker. In his senior year of high school, he invented a remote-control robot and won an invention competition. In the 1990s, Mr. Johnson was an ex-NASA engineer when he improved upon the invention of a child's toy, the water gun. His patent, U.S. Patent 4591071, allowed him to license the rights to several companies who in turn paid him millions of dollars in royalties for his water gun invention. He holds more than 40 issued patents, including one for a wet diaper detector and several for toy rockets.

Bette Nesmith Graham

Liquid Paper patent holder

Bette Nesmith Graham, a secretary and artist, used her own kitchen blender to mix up her first batch of Liquid Paper, the substance used to cover up written or typed mistakes. She then started the Mistake Out Company, which would later be renamed Liquid Paper. By 1967, it had grown into a million-dollar business. She later sold her corporation for $47.5 million! Graham educated herself on how to patent her invention, run a business, and promote and sell her product.

These people should serve as an inspiration for your future, your ideas, and your dreams. If you learn anything from reading about them, it should be that dreams do come true and that any idea, no matter how small, can make a big difference in the world.

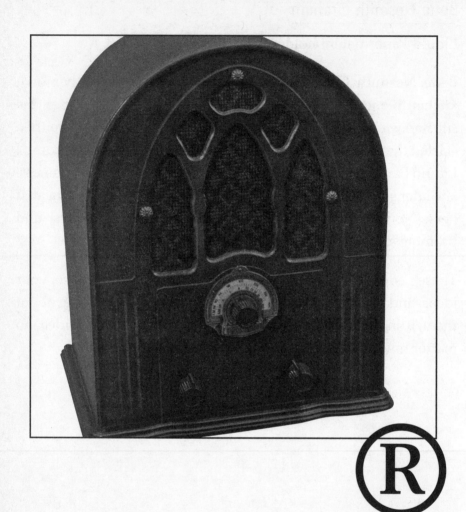

Though many people credited Guglielmo Marconi as the inventor of the radio, Nikola Telsa was actually the first to patent the invention.

Chapter 21

Patent Searches

"Excluded from such patent protection are laws of nature, physical phenomena, and abstract ideas."

Diamond v. Diehr, U. S. Supreme Court, 1981

It can eliminate a lot of time and headaches in looking for patent protection if you make sure early in your search that your patent submission does not infringe on other patent holders.

A patent search is a vigorous process. It is part of your search for prior art, which is any body of knowledge that relates to your invention. Prior art includes previous patents, trade journal articles, publications including data books and catalogs, public discussions, trade shows, or public use or sales anywhere in the world. A patent search involves searching different databases to see if your idea has already been patented, to know if you can patent your idea. Class organizes patents and subclass of invention, similar to the way books is organized in a library. By using the classification system, you can find and examine patents in the same field or class as your idea.

This period can be extended in specific circumstances. Consequently, there is always a "hidden" pool of documents that will only become available for search at a future date. A patent search is a process that entails the use and combination of large numbers of keywords and expressions, which cannot be meticulously completed in one attempt. As a result, a patent search on an idea must be executed frequently and tirelessly. Assuming you have an idea and would like to know if it is novel, the next logical step is to perform a patent search covering relevant intellectual property databases. Currently, most intellectual property organizations provide access to their databases via the World Wide Web.

A patent search proves beneficial at various periods of the inventing process. An initial patent search at the time of conception and formulation of an idea helps in evaluating the depth and degree of the field of invention. In due course, and particularly in the case of existing prior art, the patent search helps in refining the idea and encourages further inventive thinking by challenging the inventors with respect to the novelty of the idea. Finally, a comprehensive awareness of the prior art, as reflected in the "background" section of the patent submission, would aid the examiner at the patent office in assessing the technology and hurry the review process.

Patent No. 1 issued on July 13, 1836 by United States Patent and Trademark Office.

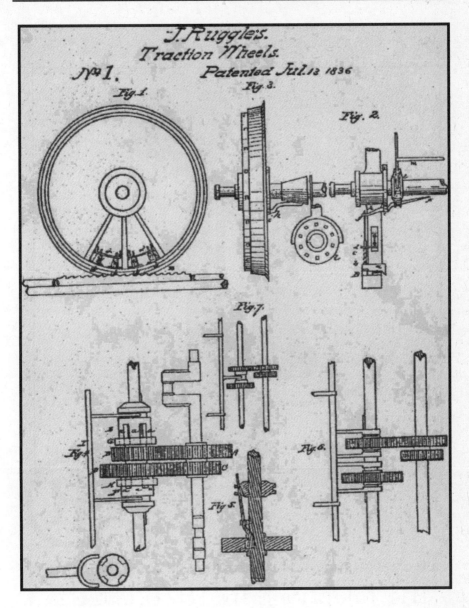

Alexander Graham Bell invented the telephone in 1876. At the time, this became known as one of the most valuable patents.

Chapter 22

The Patent
Application Process

"Scientific truth, or the mathematical expression of it, is not a patentable invention."

MR&T v. RCA, U. S. Supreme Court, 1939

A non-provisional patent application must be filed. This is the first step. The mere filing of the patent application, however, will not guarantee you will receive a patent for your invention. Once the application is filed, it is preliminarily evaluated by the United States Patent Office to establish whether all of the obligatory parts of the application are present. In order to attain a filing date, the filing must contain, at a minimum, the specification, at least one drawing (if in fact a drawing is necessary to understand the invention, which is almost always the case), and at least one claim. Once the patent-granting authority determines your idea has utility, and is novel and non-obvious, a patent may be granted.

The United States is a first-to-file nation. In a first-to-file system, the right to the grant of a patent for a given invention lies with the first person to file a patent application for protection of that invention, regardless of the date of actual invention. Therefore, invention in the U.S. is generally defined to comprise two steps: (1) conception of the invention, and (2) reduction to practice of the invention. When an inventor conceives of an invention and meticulously reduces the invention to practice, or by filing a patent application, practicing the invention, etc., the inventor's date of invention will be the date of conception.

If these three things are offered to the patent office, a filing date is awarded and the application will move forward. Notice that the filing fee, among other things, does not need to be present at the time of filing. To be sure, the United States Patent Office will not do anything substantive until you pay the filing fee, as this must be paid later. There is a fee applicable for the privilege of paying the filing fee after the initial filing. The next step in the process is frequently a restriction being issued. At the United States Patent Office you are then entitled to a single invention in an application: one fee for one invention.

Remember this advice from the United States Patent and Trademark Office: "In order for an invention to be patentable it must be new as defined in the patent law, which provides that an invention cannot be patented if: (a) the invention was known or used by others in this country, or patented or described in a printed publication in this or a foreign country, before the invention thereof by the applicant for patent, or (b) the invention was patented or described in a printed publication in this or a foreign country or in public use or on sale in this country more than one year prior to the application for patent in the United States."

If there is more than one invention present, it will be necessary to elect one invention to move forward. You can then file a divisional application on non-elected inventions without compromising your filing date. Once you have made it this far, your application is now ready to enter the examination chapter. How rapidly the examiner will get to review the application varies to a great extent depending upon the intricacy and technological area of invention. In some types of inventions it may take two or three years to hear from the examiner. In rare cases an examiner may get in touch with you within six to eight months.

The first instance you will substantively hear from the examiner is when he or she delivers what is referred to as a First Office Action. Now you are truly starting what most would refer to as prosecution. The examiner has told you what, if anything, he or she thinks is patentable, and has described what claims are missing and why.

The prosecution process sees applicants go back and forth with the examiner to persuade him or her that there is patentable subject matter. This give and take course of action does have its chronological limits. After the reply by the applicant or attorney, the examiner will issue a Second Office Action, which could be made final.

After the examiner has discarded claims twice, he or she has the power to make the rejections final. Final rejection, however, is not so conclusive. There is still a chance to amend and make changes, but the examiner must authorize the amendments and changes. Final rejection really indicates the entrance into the end game of a prosecution, whereby practically anything you want to do requires examiner approval.

After prosecution is ended you will either wind up with some claims being permitted, all being rejected, or all being allowed. In most circumstances it is probably safe to say that some claims will be permitted and some rejected. At this time you can make a number of choices. You can either have the allowed claims issue or file a Request for Continuing Examination (RCE). This RCE will resume prosecution. If you choose to have the allowed claims issued, you can opt to file a Continuation or a Continuation in Part, which will allow you to keep trying to convince the patent examiner that undeniable claims are allowable. Both Continuations and Continuations in Part start a new application process from the beginning, as opposed to the RCE, which continues on the same application. Use of the RCE, nonetheless, will prevent the allowed claims from immediately issuing.

Along the way, a decision can be made to appeal final rejection by the examiner. An appeal goes before the Board of Patent Appeals and perhaps, in due course, to the United States Court of Appeals for the Federal Circuit, or the United States District Court for the District of Columbia.

As a general rule, most appeals are not successful, which makes appealing a difficult decision unless there has been real, particular error, or the Patent Office is holding firmly to certain elucidations, which would have negative penalty for a series of patent applications.

What Can You Patent?

Generally any device, substance, method, or process can be patented. Inventions in any field of technology can be patented if they are demonstrated to be new or novel, involve an inventive step, and are industrially or utility applicable. An invention is new if it is not rendered obvious by prior art, which is considered to be: everything made accessible to the public anywhere in the world by means of written exposé, including drawings and other illustrations, or by oral disclosure, use, presentation, or other non-written methods, provided that such discovery transpired before the date of filing of the application or, if priority is claimed, before the priority date validated.

In order to be granted a patent, the invention must be original. An invention is original if it is not anticipated by prior art. This means that the invention must not have been revealed to enable the invention to be understood, by word of mouth, use, in any printed publication, or in any other way, anywhere in the world before a first application is made for a patent.

How do you establish whether an invention is novel?

Novelty is measured by transporting your searches in obtainable printed publications. These publications may comprise previous patent specifications, textbooks, technical journals, and sales brochures. Other revelations, which could illustrate that your invention is not new contain the sale of a product or its use in public. It is extremely advantageous to have a search carried out in instances where patents in foreign countries are required. This is because foreign patent applications are expensive and the likelihood of obtaining strong patents should be properly considered.

Standard Patent Application

A standard patent application is a patent application holding all of the essential parts necessary for the award of a patent. A standard patent may or may not result in the grant of a patent depending on the result of an examination by the patent office it is filed in. In the United States, a standard patent application is referred to as a non-provisional application.

Provisional Patent Applications

A provisional application provides the opportunity to place an application on file to obtain a filing date, thereby securing a priority date, but without the expense and complexity of a standard patent application. No enforceable rights can be obtained solely through the filing of a provisional application.

Continuation Patent Applications

Continuation applications can be filed as a continuation of a previous application. Such an application is a method of combining material from a previous application with a new application, when the priority year has expired and additional refinement is needed.

Divisional Patent Applications

Divisional applications are the ones, which have been divided from an existing application. A divisional application is useful if a unity of invention objection is issued.

Drawings for the Application

Drawings for a patent are among the most important information needed when applying.

PTO/SB/05 (07-07)
Approved for use through 06/30/2010. OMB 0651-0032
U.S. Patent and Trademark Office. U.S. DEPARTMENT OF COMMERCE
Under the Paperwork Reduction Act of 1995, no persons are required to respond to a collection of information unless it displays a valid OMB control number.

UTILITY
PATENT APPLICATION
TRANSMITTAL

(Only for new nonprovisional applications under 37 CFR 1.53(b))

Attorney Docket No.	
First Inventor	
Title	
Express Mail Label No.	

APPLICATION ELEMENTS
See MPEP chapter 600 concerning utility patent application contents.

ADDRESS TO: **Commissioner for Patents**
P.O. Box 1450
Alexandria VA 22313-1450

1. ☐ **Fee Transmittal Form** (e.g., PTO/SB/17)
   (Submit an original and a duplicate for fee processing)
2. ☐ **Applicant claims small entity status.**
   See 37 CFR 1.27.
3. ☐ **Specification**   [Total Pages_____]
   Both the claims and abstract must start on a new page
   (For information on the preferred arrangement, see MPEP 608.01(a))
4. ☐ **Drawing(s)** (35 U.S.C. 113) [Total Sheets _____]

5. **Oath or Declaration**   [Total Sheets _____]
   a. ☐ Newly executed (original or copy)
   b. ☐ A copy from a prior application (37 CFR 1.63(d))
      (for continuation/divisional with Box 18 completed)
      i. ☐ DELETION OF INVENTOR(S)
         Signed statement attached deleting inventor(s)
         name in the prior application, see 37 CFR
         1.63(d)(2) and 1.33(b).

6. ☐ **Application Data Sheet.** See 37 CFR 1.76

7. ☐ **CD-ROM or CD-R** in duplicate, large table or
   Computer Program *(Appendix)*
      ☐ Landscape Table on CD

8. ☐ **Nucleotide and/or Amino Acid Sequence Submission**
   (if applicable, items a. – c. are required)
   a. ☐ Computer Readable Form (CRF)
   b. ☐ Specification Sequence Listing on:

      i. ☐ CD-ROM or CD-R (2 copies); or
      ii. ☐ Paper

   c. ☐ Statements verifying identity of above copies

ACCOMPANYING APPLICATION PARTS

9. ☐ **Assignment Papers** (cover sheet (PTO-1595) & document(s))

   Name of Assignee_____

10. ☐ **37 CFR 3.73(b) Statement**   ☐ **Power of**
    (when there is an assignee)   **Attorney**

11. ☐ **English Translation Document** *(if applicable)*

12. ☐ **Information Disclosure Statement** (PTO/SB/08 or PTO-1449)
       ☐ Copies of foreign patent documents,
          publications, & other information

13. ☐ **Preliminary Amendment**

14. ☐ **Return Receipt Postcard** (MPEP 503)
       (Should be specifically itemized)

15. ☐ **Certified Copy of Priority Document(s)**
       (if foreign priority is claimed)

16. ☐ **Nonpublication Request** under 35 U.S.C. 122(b)(2)(B)(i).
       Applicant must attach form PTO/SB/35 or equivalent.

17. ☐ **Other:**_____
       _____

18. If a CONTINUING APPLICATION, check appropriate box, and supply the requisite information below and in the first sentence of the specification following the title, or in an Application Data Sheet under 37 CFR 1.76:

☐ Continuation   ☐ Divisional   ☐ Continuation-in-part (CIP)   of prior application No.: ....

Prior application information: Examiner _____   Art Unit: _____

19. CORRESPONDENCE ADDRESS

☐ The address associated with Customer Number: [   ]   **OR** ☐ Correspondence address below

Name	
Address	

City		State		Zip Code	
Country		Telephone		Email	

Signature		Date	
Name (Print/Type)		Registration No. (Attorney/Agent)	

This collection of information is required by 37 CFR 1.53(b). The information is required to obtain or retain a benefit by the public which is to file (and by the USPTO to process) an application. Confidentiality is governed by 35 U.S.C. 122 and 37 CFR 1.11 and 1.14. This collection is estimated to take 12 minutes to complete, including gathering, preparing, and submitting the completed application form to the USPTO. Time will vary depending upon the individual case. Any comments on the amount of time you require to complete this form and/or suggestions for reducing this burden, should be sent to the Chief Information Officer, U.S. Patent and Trademark Office, U.S. Department of Commerce, P.O. Box 1450, Alexandria, VA 22313-1450. DO NOT SEND FEES OR COMPLETED FORMS TO THIS ADDRESS. **SEND TO: Commissioner for Patents, P.O. Box 1450, Alexandria, VA 22313-1450.**
If you need assistance in completing the form, call 1-800-PTO-9199 and select option 2.

PTO/SB/19 (07-07)
Approved for use through 06/30/2010. OMB 0651-0032
U.S. Patent and Trademark Office; U.S. DEPARTMENT OF COMMERCE
Under the Paperwork Reduction Act of 1995, no persons are required to respond to a collection of information unless it displays a valid OMB control number.

PLANT PATENT APPLICATION TRANSMITTAL	Attorney Docket No.	
	First Named Inventor	
	Title	
(Only for new nonprovisional applications filed under 37 CFR 1.53(b))	Express Mail Label No.	

ADDRESS TO:
Commissioner for Patents
P.O. Box 1450
Alexandria, VA 22313-1450

APPLICATION ELEMENTS
See MPEP chapters 600 & 1600 concerning plant patent application contents.

1. ☐ Fee Transmittal Form *(e.g., PTO/SB/17)*
   (Submit an original, and a duplicate for fee processing)
2. ☐ Applicant claims small entity status. See 37 CFR 1.27.
3. ☐ Specification   [Total Pages _____]
   (preferred arrangement set forth below)
   - Descriptive title of the invention
   - Cross References to Related Applications
   - Statement Regarding Fed sponsored R & D
   - Latin name of genus and species
   - Variety denomination
   - Background of the Invention
   - Brief Description of the Drawings
   - Detailed Botanical Description
   - A single claim
   - Abstract of the Disclosure
4. ☐ Color drawing(s)   [Total Sheets _____]
   (2 copies required – 37 CFR 1.165(b))
5. ☐ Oath or Declaration   [Total Pages _____]
   a. ☐ Newly executed (original or copy)
   b. ☐ A copy from a prior application (37 CFR 1.63(d))
      (for continuation/divisional with Box 16 completed)
      i ☐ DELETION OF INVENTOR(S)
        Signed statement attached deleting
        inventor(s) named in the prior application,
        see 37 CFR 1.63(d)(2) and 1.33(b).
6. ☐ Application Data Sheet. See 37 CFR 1.76.

ACCOMPANYING APPLICATION PARTS

7. ☐ Assignment Papers (cover sheet & document(s))
8. ☐ 37 CFR 3.73(b) Statement   ☐ Power of
   (when there is an assignee)   Attorney
9. ☐ English Translation Document *(if applicable)*
10. ☐ Information Disclosure Statement (IDS)
    PTO/SB/08 or PTO-1449
    ☐ Copies of foreign patent documents, NPL &
       Pending U.S. patent applications
11. ☐ Preliminary Amendment
12. ☐ Return Receipt Postcard (MPEP 503)
    (Should be specifically itemized)
13. ☐ Certified Copy of Priority Document(s)
    (if foreign priority is claimed)
14. ☐ Request Nonpublication under 35 U.S.C. 122(b)(2)(B)(i)
    Applicant must attach form PTO/SB/35 or equivalent.
15. ☐ Other:

Note: Please state the Latin name and variety denomination of the plant claimed in a separate section of the specification.

16. If a CONTINUING APPLICATION, check appropriate box, and supply the requisite information below and in the first sentence of the specification following the title, or in an Application Data Sheet under 37 CFR 1.76.

☐ Continuation   ☐ Divisional   ☐ Continuation-in-part (CIP) of prior application No.: _____

Prior application information: Examiner _____   Art Unit: _____

17. CORRESPONDENCE ADDRESS

☐ The address associated with Customer Number: _____   **OR**   ☐ Correspondence address below

Name	
Address	

City		State		Zip Code	
Country		Telephone		Email	

Signature		Date	
Name (Print/Typed)		Registration No.	

If you need assistance in completing the form, call 1-800-PTO-9199 and select option 2.

PTO/SB/18 (07-07)
Approved for use through 06/30/2010. OMB 0651-0032
U.S. Patent and Trademark Office; U.S. DEPARTMENT OF COMMERCE
Under the Paperwork Reduction Act of 1995, no persons are required to respond to a collection of information unless it displays a valid OMB control number.

DESIGN PATENT APPLICATION TRANSMITTAL

(Only for new nonprovisional applications under 37 CFR 1.53(b))

Attorney Docket No.	
First Named Inventor	
Title	
Express Mail Label No.	

ADDRESS TO:
Commissioner for Patents
P.O. Box 1450
Alexandria, VA 22313-1450

DESIGN V. UTILITY: A "design patent" protects an article's ornamental appearance (e.g., the way an article looks) (35 U.S.C. 171), while a "utility patent" protects the way an article is used and works (35 U.S.C. 101). The ornamental appearance of an article includes its shape/configuration or surface ornamentation upon the article, or both. Both a design and a utility patent may be obtained on an article if invention resides both in its ornamental appearance and its utility. For more information, see MPEP 1502.01.

APPLICATION ELEMENTS
See MPEP 1500 concerning design patent application contents.

1. ☐ Fee Transmittal Form *(e.g., PTO/SB/17)*
   (Submit an original, and a duplicate for fee processing)

2. ☐ Applicant claims small entity status.
   See 37 CFR 1.27.

3. ☐ Specification   *[Total Pages _____]*
   (preferred arrangement set forth below, MPEP 1503.01)
   - Preamble
   - Cross References to Related Applications
   - Statement Regarding Fed sponsored R & D
   - Description of the figure(s) of the drawings
   - Feature description
   - Claim (only one (1) claim permitted, MPEP 1503.03)

4. ☐ Drawing(s) *(37 CFR 1.152) [Total Sheets _____]*

5. Oath or Declaration   *[Total Pages _____]*

   a. ☐ Newly executed (original or copy)

   b. ☐ A copy from a prior application (37 CFR 1.63(d))
      (for continuation/divisional with Box 16 completed)
      DELETION OF INVENTOR(S)
      i. ☐ Signed statement attached deleting
         inventor(s) named in the prior application,
         see 37 CFR 1.63(d)(2) and 1.33(b)

6. ☐ Application Data Sheet. See 37 CFR 1.76

ACCOMPANYING APPLICATION PARTS

7. ☐ Assignment Papers (cover sheet & document(s))

8. ☐ 37 CFR 3.73(b) Statement   ☐ Power of
   (when there is an assignee)   Attorney

9. ☐ English Translation Document *(if applicable)*

10. ☐ Information Disclosure Statement (IDS)
    PTO/SB/08 or PTO-1449
    ☐ Copies of foreign patent documents,
       publications, & other information

11. ☐ Preliminary Amendment

12. ☐ Return Receipt Postcard (MPEP 503)
    (Should be specifically itemized)

13. ☐ Certified Copy of Priority Document(s)
    (if foreign priority is claimed)

14. ☐ Request for Expedited Examination of a Design Application
    (37 CFR 1.155) (NOTE: Use "Mail Stop Expedited Design")

15. ☐ Other:

16. If a CONTINUING APPLICATION, check appropriate box, and supply the requisite information below and in the first sentence of the specification following the title, or in an Application Data Sheet under 37 CFR 1.76:

☐ Continuation   ☐ Divisional   ☐ Continuation-in-part (CIP) of prior application No.: _____

Prior application information: Examiner _____ *Art Unit:* _____

17. CORRESPONDENCE ADDRESS

☐ The address associated with
  Customer Number: [_____]   **OR**   ☐ Correspondence address below

Name	
Address	

City		State		Zip Code	
Country		Telephone		Email	

Signature		Date	
Name (Print/Type)		Registration No. (Attorney/Agent)	

This collection of information is required by 37 CFR 1.53(b). The information is required to obtain or retain a benefit by the public which is to file (and by the USPTO to process) an application. Confidentiality is governed by 35 U.S.C. 122 and 37 CFR 1.11 and 1.14. This collection is estimated to take 12 minutes to complete, including gathering, preparing, and submitting the completed application form to the USPTO. Time will vary depending upon the individual case. Any comments on the amount of time you require to complete this form and/or suggestions for reducing this burden, should be sent to the Chief Information Officer, U.S. Patent and Trademark Office, U.S. Department of Commerce, P.O. Box 1450, Alexandria, VA 22313-1450. DO NOT SEND FEES OR COMPLETED FORMS TO THIS ADDRESS. **SEND TO: Commissioner for Patents, P.O. Box 1450, Alexandria, VA 22313-1450.**
If you need assistance in completing the form, call 1-800-PTO-9199 and select option 2.

PTO/SB/16 (10-07)
Approved for use through 06/30/2010. OMB 0651-0032
U.S. Patent and Trademark Office; U.S. DEPARTMENT OF COMMERCE
Under the Paperwork Reduction Act of 1995, no persons are required to respond to a collection of information unless it displays a valid OMB control number.

PROVISIONAL APPLICATION FOR PATENT COVER SHEET – Page 1 of 2

This is a request for filing a PROVISIONAL APPLICATION FOR PATENT under 37 CFR 1.53(c).

Express Mail Label No. _____

INVENTOR(S)

Given Name (first and middle [if any])	Family Name or Surname	Residence (City and either State or Foreign Country)

Additional inventors are being named on the _____ separately numbered sheets attached hereto

TITLE OF THE INVENTION (500 characters max):

Direct all correspondence to: **CORRESPONDENCE ADDRESS**

☐ The address corresponding to Customer Number: _____

OR

☐ Firm or Individual Name

Address

City	State	Zip
Country	Telephone	Email

ENCLOSED APPLICATION PARTS (check all that apply)

☐ Application Data Sheet. See 37 CFR 1.76   ☐ CD(s), Number of CDs _____

☐ Drawing(s) *Number of Sheets* _____   ☐ Other (specify) _____

☐ Specification (e.g. description of the invention) *Number of Pages* _____

Fees Due: Filing Fee of $210 ($105 for small entity). If the specification and drawings exceed 100 sheets of paper, an application size fee is also due, which is $260 ($130 for small entity) for each additional 50 sheets or fraction thereof. See 35 U.S.C. 41(a)(1)(G) and 37 CFR 1.16(s).

METHOD OF PAYMENT OF THE FILING FEE AND APPLICATION SIZE FEE FOR THIS PROVISIONAL APPLICATION FOR PATENT

☐ Applicant claims small entity status. See 37 CFR 1.27.

☐ A check or money order is enclosed to cover the filing fee and application size fee (if applicable).

☐ Payment by credit card. Form PTO-2038 is attached   **TOTAL FEE AMOUNT ($)**

☐ The Director is hereby authorized to charge the filing fee and application size fee (if applicable) or credit any overpayment to Deposit

Account Number: _____. A duplicative copy of this form is enclosed for fee processing.

USE ONLY FOR FILING A PROVISIONAL APPLICATION FOR PATENT

This collection of information is required by 37 CFR 1.51. The information is required to obtain or retain a benefit by the public which is to file (and by the USPTO to process) an application. Confidentiality is governed by 35 U.S.C. 122 and 37 CFR 1.11 and 1.14. This collection is estimated to take 8 hours to complete, including gathering, preparing, and submitting the completed application form to the USPTO. Time will vary depending upon the individual case. Any comments on the amount of time you require to complete this form and/or suggestions for reducing this burden, should be sent to the Chief Information Officer, U.S. Patent and Trademark Office, U.S. Department of Commerce, P.O. Box 1450, Alexandria, VA 22313-1450. DO NOT SEND FEES OR COMPLETED FORMS TO THIS ADDRESS. **SEND TO: Commissioner for Patents, P.O. Box 1450, Alexandria, VA 22313-1450.**
If you need assistance in completing the form, call 1-800-PTO-9199 and select option 2.

PROVISIONAL APPLICATION COVER SHEET

PTO/SB/16 (10-07)

Approved for use through 06/30/2010. OMB 0651-0032

U.S. Patent and Trademark Office; U.S. DEPARTMENT OF COMMERCE

Under the Paperwork Reduction Act of 1995, no persons are required to respond to a collection of information unless it displays a valid OMB control number.

The invention was made by an agency of the United States Government or under a contract with an agency of the United States Government.

☐ No.

☐ Yes, the name of the U.S. Government agency and the Government contract number are: _____

_____

WARNING:

Petitioner/applicant is cautioned to avoid submitting personal information in documents filed in a patent application that may contribute to identity theft. Personal information such as social security numbers, bank account numbers, or credit card numbers (other than a check or credit card authorization form PTO-2038 submitted for payment purposes) is never required by the USPTO to support a petition or an application. If this type of personal information is included in documents submitted to the USPTO, petitioners/applicants should consider redacting such personal information from the documents before submitting them to the USPTO. Petitioner/applicant is advised that the record of a patent application is available to the public after publication of the application (unless a non-publication request in compliance with 37 CFR 1.213(a) is made in the application) or issuance of a patent. Furthermore, the record from an abandoned application may also be available to the public if the application is referenced in a published application or an issued patent (see 37 CFR 1.14). Checks and credit card authorization forms PTO-2038 submitted for payment purposes are not retained in the application file and therefore are not publicly available.

SIGNATURE_____Date_____

TYPED or PRINTED NAME _____REGISTRATION NO. _____

(if appropriate)

TELEPHONE _____ Docket Number:_____

PRIVACY ACT STATEMENT

The Privacy Act of 1974 (P.L. 93-579) requires that you be given certain information in connection with your submission of the attached form related to a patent application or patent. Accordingly, pursuant to the requirements of the Act, please be advised that: (1) the general authority for the collection of this information is 35 U.S.C. 2(b)(2); (2) furnishing of the information solicited is voluntary; and (3) the principal purpose for which the information is used by the U.S. Patent and Trademark Office is to process and/or examine your submission related to a patent application or patent. If you do not furnish the requested information, the U.S. Patent and Trademark Office may not be able to process and/or examine your submission, which may result in termination of proceedings or abandonment of the application or expiration of the patent.

The information provided by you in this form will be subject to the following routine uses:

1. The information on this form will be treated confidentially to the extent allowed under the Freedom of Information Act (5 U.S.C. 552) and the Privacy Act (5 U.S.C 552a). Records from this system of records may be disclosed to the Department of Justice to determine whether disclosure of these records is required by the Freedom of Information Act.

2. A record from this system of records may be disclosed, as a routine use, in the course of presenting evidence to a court, magistrate, or administrative tribunal, including disclosures to opposing counsel in the course of settlement negotiations.

3. A record in this system of records may be disclosed, as a routine use, to a Member of Congress submitting a request involving an individual, to whom the record pertains, when the individual has requested assistance from the Member with respect to the subject matter of the record.

4. A record in this system of records may be disclosed, as a routine use, to a contractor of the Agency having need for the information in order to perform a contract. Recipients of information shall be required to comply with the requirements of the Privacy Act of 1974, as amended, pursuant to 5 U.S.C. 552a(m).

5. A record related to an International Application filed under the Patent Cooperation Treaty in this system of records may be disclosed, as a routine use, to the International Bureau of the World Intellectual Property Organization, pursuant to the Patent Cooperation Treaty.

PRIVACY ACT STATEMENT

6. A record in this system of records may be disclosed, as a routine use, to another federal agency for purposes of National Security review (35 U.S.C. 181) and for review pursuant to the Atomic Energy Act (42 U.S.C. 218(c)).

7. A record from this system of records may be disclosed, as a routine use, to the Administrator, General Services, or his/her designee, during an inspection of records conducted by GSA as part of that agency's responsibility to recommend improvements in records management practices and programs, under authority of 44 U.S.C. 2904 and 2906. Such disclosure shall be made in accordance with the GSA regulations governing inspection of records for this purpose, and any other relevant (i.e., GSA or Commerce) directive. Such disclosure shall not be used to make determinations about individuals.

8. A record from this system of records may be disclosed, as a routine use, to the public after either publication of the application pursuant to 35 U.S.C. 122(b) or issuance of a patent pursuant to 35 U.S.C. 151. Further, a record may be disclosed, subject to the limitations of 37 CFR 1.14, as a routine use, to the public if the record was filed in an application which became abandoned or in which the proceedings were terminated and which application is referenced by either a published application, an application open to public inspection or an issued patent.

9. A record from this system of records may be disclosed, as a routine use, to a Federal, State, or local law enforcement agency, if the USPTO becomes aware of a violation or potential violation of law or regulation.

Divisional Applications

A divisional patent application is an application claiming priority from some previously filed patent application in which more than one invention was disclosed. The divisional application has claims directed to a different invention than that claimed in the parent application. The most common way this happens is that the Patent Office rules that your application contains more than one invention, communicating this in what is called a restriction requirement. The applicant then elects to pursue one of the inventions in that application.

Provisional Applications

A provisional application is an affordable way for the small inventor to get started on the road to fully protecting his/her invention. It provides applicants a quick and easy way to establish an early effective filing date in a patent application, allowing the term "Patent Pending" to be applied. What is very important is that it provides the inventor 12 months to further develop the invention.

Non-Provisional (Utility) Applications

Utility patents are granted to anyone who invents or discovers a new and useful process, machine, manufacture, or composition of matter, or any new and useful improvement thereof. "Process" means a process or method. "Manufacture" refers to articles, which are made. "Composition of matter" relates to chemical compositions and may include mixtures of ingredients as well as new chemical compounds. A utility patent has a term of 20 years from the application date.

Continuation Applications

Under United States patent practice, a continuation patent application is an application which claims priority from an application previously filed. A continuation application is usually filed when the Patent Office has responded to the parent application with a final office action, but the applicant wishes to revise the claims again. A continuation application receives the priority date of its parent application. A continuation application is often filed using the file wrapper continuation (FWC) administrative procedure.

Foreign Patents

Countries outside the United States account for about two-thirds of the total world market, especially in high technology products. A company wanting to commercialize university technology will want to sell that technology in as many national markets as it can in order to maximize profit. Even when the only market being considered is the U.S. market, lack of foreign patent protection may invite "pirates" to set up business in other countries and illegally import these goods into the United States. Most companies prefer that foreign patent rights be as prosecutable as United States patent rights.

Patent Prosecution

There are several ways to fight the patent office if you feel your patent was not received. Patent prosecution describes the communication between applicants or their representative and a patent office with regard to a patent or an application for a patent. Generally, patent prosecution can be divided into pre-grant prosecution, which entails negotiation with a patent office for the grant of a patent, and post-grant prosecution, which involves a number of issues such as post-grant amendment and opposition. Patent prosecution is separate from patent litigation, which depicts legal action relating to the infringement of patents.

Patent prosecution communicates the process of applying for a United States patent and having the patent examined by the United States Patent Office. There are many multifaceted legal and technical requirements that must be satisfied in order to get not only an issued patent, but also a valuable patent that includes general claims and is protected from defects or serious limitations.

It is significant to note in advance that no one can guarantee that any patent claims will be permitted or a patent will issue. The patent prosecution phase can typically take two to three years from the filing date of the utility application, although it may be extended or shortened depending upon the situations.

Instructions: Provide the following information and promptly confer with your attorney to develop a proper course of action.

INVENTION DISCLOSURE FORM FOR UTILITY PATENT APPLICATION EXAMPLE

Descriptive Title:_____

Inventor:_____ Tel/Fax/E-mail _____

Address: _____ Citizenship: _____

(Include same information for co-inventors if applicable)

Employer: _____

Address: _____

1. What is the problem solved by the invention?_____

_____

2. How was the problem solved before the invention?_____

_____

3. Describe the invention — list and/or attach all relevant information (i.e. specifications and drawings): _____

_____

Utility — What does the invention do? _____

_____

Method — What functional steps does the invention perform? _____

_____

INVENTION DISCLOSURE FORM FOR UTILITY PATENT APPLICATION EXAMPLE

Novel Features — What are the features of the invention that distinguish it from other known solutions to the problem being solved? _____

_____

Benefits — What positive or unexpected results are provided by the invention? ___

_____

4. The invention was first conceived on (date)_____

5. A prototype was completed and demonstrated on (date)_____

6. The invention was first published or otherwise disclosed on (date) _____

(Describe nature of disclosure) _____

_____

7. The invention was first sold or offered for sale on (date)_____

INVENTION DISCLOSURE FORM FOR DESIGN PATENT APPLICATION EXAMPLE

(Describe nature of sale or offer for sale) _____

Instructions: Provide the following information and promptly confer with your attorney to develop a proper course of action.

Descriptive Title of Article: _____

Brief Reference to Design Features: _____

Inventor: _____ Tel/Fax/E-mail _____

Address: _____ Citizenship: _____

(Include same information for co-inventors if applicable)

Employer: _____

Address: _____

INVENTION DISCLOSURE FORM FOR DESIGN PATENT APPLICATION EXAMPLE

1. Form — How is invention constructed? What does it look like?

Attach photos or drawings: _____

_____

2. Purpose — What does invention do? What is it for? What structural features are essential/functional? _____

_____

3. Ornamentation— What non-functional elements of the design and shape are being claimed as novel and non-obvious? _____

_____

4. The shape and design was first conceived on (date): _____

5. A prototype was completed and demonstrated on (date): _____

6. The final article design was disclosed, advertised or offered for sale on: _____

Chapter 23

_____

Patent Infringement

"Well, that's what it was bloody well designed to do, wasn't it?"

Frank Whittle, English inventor

The word "infringement" means a violation upon the domain belonging to a patentee that is explained by the claims of the patent. If a patent is analogized to real property, the claims communicate to the boundary recited in the deed. Invasion of the boundary of a landowner's real estate is called trespass, while incursion of a patentee's claims is called infringement. Patent infringement is a serious offense in the United States. It can lead to serious damage awards if the case goes to trial.

What Is Patent Infringement?

This happens when someone uses, sells, makes, offers for sale, or imports a patented invention without consent from the patent owner. Offering to sell a patented invention in the United States or one of its territories is considered patent infringement.

The most obvious form of it is a company that creates the same product as a previously patented product and markets it as their own. It can occur in several ways. Another company introduces a candy that does not necessarily encourage weight loss, but the packaging of the candy induces the consumer to believe the product is the same or similar to the initial weight loss candy. This is known as induced patent infringement. Induced patent infringement relies on the principle that the company does not need to actually create a product that infringes on the patent rights; it only has to be presented to the consumer as a patent infringement.

Patent infringement on a patent pending product is truly a matter of legal hair splitting. If a patent is pending, it does fall under protection. Patent infringement on a patent pending item can happen accidentally; nevertheless, most products marketed under a pending patent are marked with a "Patent Pending" noticeable wording. Whether it happens unintentionally or with deceitful intent, patent infringement can be a serious offense. Intentional patent infringement, or willful patent infringement, as it is better known, can bear extremely high damages awards. Willful patent infringement is repeatedly committed with full knowledge and an intentionally deceitful marketing plan. This can include pretending the product is original through packaging, advertisement, or even ingredient labeling. Willful infringement cases are serious and have closed companies due to the award damages in court. Patent infringement laws do help to better our society by providing financial motivation for creative individuals to create products that make the world a better, safer place.

When Can a Patent Be Infringed?

Only during the term of the patent. In order to bring an infringement action against someone or a company, you as the patent holder have a limit of six years from the date of the infringement. Litigation proceeds like any other federal court case, and the determination can come from the judge or a jury.

What Is Willful Infringement?

Legally, this refers to the opinion of counsel, where if an suspected patent infringer did not supply or get opinion of counsel as to the use of an infringing invention, the courts would conclude that such an opinion would have been adverse, which led to a beyond-question resolution of willful infringement. Now, with the Court of Appeals for the Federal Circuit reversing this 20-year-old precedent, stating that the absence of an opinion of counsel is only one of numerous factors to be considered when formulating if a patent infringement is willful.

Patent Terminology

Abstract

The abstract is a concise, one-paragraph summary of the patent detailing the structure, nature, and purpose of the invention.

Art or prior art

A term used in consideration of the problem of patentable novelty encompassing all that is known prior to the filing date of the application in the particular field of the invention, represented by already-issued patents and publications.

Assignee

The assignee is the recipient of the patent rights. The assignee may be a U.S. or foreign company or individual of the U.S. or a foreign government. The assignee is not necessarily the inventor of the invention being patented. Many inventors assign the rights to their inventions over to other individuals or institutions.

Basic patent or pioneer patent

This is a broad patent that is the first in a given area.

Best mode

The best mode is the inventor's preferred and principal method of representing the invention.

Broad claim

A broad claim is a statement in a patent describing extensive variations of the invention. Such a statement usually includes a broad range of alternatives by its implication without using an alternative form of presentation.

Business incubator

This is a program that assists entrepreneurs to develop a business. The primary features are flexible and affordable space, access to shared office services, professional business management assistance, and a supportive entrepreneurial environment.

Classification of subjects

The Patent and Trademark Office (PTO) has developed a system of classification so that its subject matter can locate a patent: what a device does, what composition a chemical has, etc. The system consists of over 400 classes and 100,000 subclasses, which are continuously being revised to reflect changing technologies. It is important to have a good understanding of the classification system in order to be able to conduct a useful patent search, as it is the main point of access for locating patents in any particular area of technology.

CIP

Abbreviation for "Continuation-in-Part." When one wishes to add new material to a pending patent application, the resulting application is referred to as a CIP.

Conception

Conception is the mental portion of inventing — how the invention was formulated or a problem was solved.

Continuing patent application

This is a patent application, which follows and claims priority to an earlier filed patent application.

Contributory infringement

This refers to aiding another in infringing a patent (i.e. selling the infringer an essential portion required for the completed infringing device, material, article, or process).

Date of invention

The earliest possible date the inventor either filed the patent application or the date the inventor can prove the invention was built and tested in the United States.

Declaration

A statement executed in a patent application stating, among other things, that the applicant has made the invention described therein.

Design patent

This is a patent granted on the ornamental design of a functional item. Design patents are a type of industrial design right.

Disclosure

A statement indicating the character of an invention, its construction, operation, and application. A full disclosure is a statement sufficient to indicate, to a person skilled in the art, the necessary information to practice an invention.

Doctrine of assignor estoppel or equivalents

This is an equitable equivalent barring a patent's seller or assignor from attacking the patent's validity if he/she is found to have infringed that patent. The exclusive right of a patent is negotiable. Though the inventor's name remains unchanged, the inventor is allowed to sell the exclusive right to another party or assignee.

Doctrine of inherency

This is a vague doctrine, which includes contradicting case law. The doctrine revolves around the question of novelty and arises when an inventor tries to obtain a product patent for a product that had been unintentionally invented earlier.

Double patenting

This refers to when an applicant for a patent has filed a second application containing the same invention.

Due diligence terms

An investigation undertaken in the course of an intellectual property transaction to verify and determine the ownership and scope of intellectual property legal rights being sold, licensed, or used as collateral. The purpose of a due diligence investigation is to provide the data needed to analyze and assess the business and legal risks associated with the intellectual property rights that are the subject of the transaction.

Enablement

Enablement is the disclosure of technical information that facilitates the creation of an operating version of an invention.

Examination

An examination is the study of a patent application in the U.S. Patent and Trademark Office to determine whether or not it is in proper form and of such a character that the invention described therein can be patented.

Examiner

An examiner is an official of the U.S. Patent and Trademark Office whose responsibility is to pass on the patentability of patent applications.

Exclusive license

This is an agreement granting one party exclusive rights under an issued patent, with the licensor giving up by the terms of the license the right to offer and give a license to any other party.

Field of use license

This is a license to rights in intellectual property, limited to defined use.

Final rejection

Final rejection is the USPTO's final opinion as to the patentability of an invention.

First to file / first to invent

These are legal concepts that define who has the right to the grant of a patent for an invention. The first to file system is used in the majority of countries, with the notable exception of the United States, which operates a first to invent system.

First office action

This refers to the response from the patent examiner after the initial examination of the application.

Final office action

The examiner's answer to the applicant's or inventor's first amendment, this is supposed to end the prosecution phase. However, a final action is rarely final.

First sale doctrine

The first unrestricted sale of a patented item exhausts the patentee's control over that particular item. It generally is asserted as an affirmative defense to charges of patent infringement, but less commonly is asserted affirmatively in a declaratory judgment action.

Flash of genius test

This was a test for patentability used by the United States Federal Courts for over a decade.

Indirect infringement

Indirect infringement occurs when someone is convinced to make, use, or sell a patented invention without permission.

Industrial applicability

Industrial applicability refers to the requirement of many patent systems, which require that an invention be capable of industrial applicability in order for a patent to be granted for that invention.

Information disclosure statement (IDS)

This refers to a submission of relevant background art or information to the United States Patent and Trademark Office (USPTO) by an applicant for a patent during the patent prosecution process.

Infringement

This happens when there is a literal copy of a patented invention, or one that performs to a large extent the same function in substantially the same manner as a patented invention.

Inoperativeness

It is the failure of the invention to work due to either mechanical or methodical imperfections, or due to incomplete or erroneous description of the invention in the disclosure.

Interference

This is a proceeding the USPTO offers when two or more applicants are claiming the same invention. This can be costly.

Intellectual property rights (IPR) hygiene

Intellectual property rights hygiene is the process of ensuring that all sponsors of research are credited or compensated when that research results in intellectual property protection and licensing.

Inventive step

This is a patentability requirement according to which an invention should be sufficiently inventive (i.e. non-obvious, in order to be patented).

Inventor's notebook

It is used by inventors, scientists, and engineers to record ideas, invention process, experimental tests, results, and observations.

Joint inventor

A joint inventor is one of two or more who make joint inventive contributions to an invention.

Letters patent

This is an old term for a patent, used in reference to a bound formal copy of a patent provided by the USPTO to the inventor.

Licensee

The licensee is the entity granted rights to intellectual property by the owner of that property.

Licensor

The owner of intellectual property, which grants rights to another (the licensee) through a license.

Maintenance

The patent fees due at four, eight, and 12 years needed to keep a U. S. utility or plant patent in force for its full life.

Materials transfer agreement

This is an agreement that provides the understanding that the materials are made available only for scientific work.

Non-exclusive license

A non-exclusive license is a grant under a patent with reservation by the licensor to make a similar grant to others.

Non-obviousness

Non-obviousness is the patentability requirement according to which an invention should be non-obvious in order to be patented.

Notice of allowance

When the Patent Examiner has determined that a patent application has met the statutory requirements for patentability, the U.S. Patent and Trademark Office will issue a "Notice of Allowance." This indicates that the patent will "issue" at some future date.

Novelty

Novelty refers to a patentability requirement according to which an invention is not patentable if it was already known before the date of filing.

Office action

This is a formal report from a Patent Office examiner to an inventor or attorney detailing which claims in a patent application were allowed for later issue (publication) in a patent and which claims were rejected. The examiner gives reasons for allowance or rejection.

On-sale bar

This refers to a concept of U.S. law in which the grant of a patent is prevented if the invention that is the subject of the patent application was on sale more than one year before the priority date.

Patent application

Patent application refers to paperwork that describes an invention suitable for filing at the USPTO.

Patent family

This is a group of patents related by a common priority claim.

Patent flooding

This is patenting every possible way of doing something.

Patent infringement

This is a violation of the rights secured by a patent.

Patent misuse

The defense in patent infringement that puts a stop to a patent owner who has abused patent law from enforcing patent rights.

Patent pending

This is the time between filing a patent application and the issue of the patent. Also known as the "pendency period."

Patent prosecution

This is the process of which a patent is shepherded through the USPTO.

Patent troll

Patent troll is the pejorative term for patent holding company.

Patent watch

Patent watch refers to a process for monitoring newly issued patents on a periodic basis to see if any of these patents might be of interest.

Patentability

Patentability is a set of substantive requirements for a patent to be granted.

Petition to make special

A United States patent law procedure that requests the U.S. Patent and Trademark Office to accelerate a patent's prosecution, based on a showing that certain conditions are met.

Priority right

Priority right is the right to claim priority from an earlier application. Claiming priority gives the later-filed application a priority date of the filing date of the earlier application.

Provisional patent application (PPA)

This is an interim document that clearly explains how to make and use the invention. It is equivalent to a reproduction to practice.

PTO

PTO is the abbreviation for the United States Patent and Trademark Office. Also in common use is USPTO.

Reasonable and non-discriminatory licensing

This is a type of licensing typically used during standardization processes.

Request for continuing examination (RCE)

An RCE is a paper filed when a patent applicant wishes to continue prosecuting an application that has received Final Office Action.

Royalty

A royalty is a payment for use of an invention, usually a stated percentage of sales.

Specification

This is the written description of an invention describing the invention in sufficient enough detail that another person could duplicate it.

Subject inventions

This means any invention that is conceived or first actually reduced to practice in the performance of work under a funding agreement.

Submarine patent

A patent first published and granted long after the original application was filed is called a submarine patent.

Sufficiency of disclosure

This is an important requirement to be met by a patent in order to be validly granted.

Statutory invention registration (SIR)

This is a document permitting keeping another from getting a valid patent on the same invention if an application is discarded.

Swear back of a reference

This is a procedure under U.S. patent law whereby an inventor can get a patent even if the invention has become public before the patent application was filed.

Technology Licensing

This refers to the process by which patentable intellectual property is made marketable and is licensed or otherwise disposed for use by the public.

Term of patent

The term of patent is the maximum period during which it can be maintained in force.

Transfer

A transfer is an operation by which ownership of a patent or patent application changes (i.e. as a result of a financial transaction).

Unity of invention

This is a requirement that a patent application can relate only to one invention.

Unpatentable

Unpatentable is a description of an invention not involving sufficient departure from what was known before in the art or that for some other reason is not the proper subject matter of a patent.

USPTO

The common abbreviation for the United States Patent and Trademark Office.

Utility

Utility is a patentability requirement mainly used to prevent the patenting of inoperative devices such as perpetual motion machines.

Work-for-hire

When one is specifically hired to complete a task, such as write a discrete computer program, the resulting product is said to be a work-for-hire and thus is owned by the individual or organization that paid for the work.

Chapter 24

Utility Model Patents

"There is an eve' widening gulf between the decisions of the Patent Office in granting patents and decisions of the courts who pass upon their validity."

Report of the [U. S.] National Patent Planning Commission, 1943

What is a utility model? What does it mean to the inventor? How does it protect the inventor? Here we will answer questions regarding the utility model.

A utility model is a statutory monopoly granted for a limited time in exchange for an inventor providing sufficient teaching of his or her invention to permit a person of ordinary skill in the relevant art to perform the invention. "Until just over a decade ago, a utility model protection was regarded as being something of a curiosity in the intellectual property world" (Richards, John). The rights conferred by utility model laws are very similar to those granted by patent laws, but are more suited to what may be considered as "incremental inventions" (U. Suthersanen, Incremental Inventions in Europe: A Legal and Economic Appraisal of Second Tier Patents, in Journal of Business Law, 2001, 319 ff).

Terms such as "petty patent," "innovation patent," "minor patent," and "small patent" may also be considered to fall within the definition of "utility model" (Kelsey Martin Mott, "The Concept of the Small Patent," in *The International Business Executive*, February 5, 2007, Volume 5, Issue 3, pp. 23-24). Most inventions meet the criteria for a utility model patent, as long as they offer something novel or new and are non-obvious.

There are other types of inventions that will not meet the criteria for a patent, no matter how new they may be. For example, mathematical formulas, laws of nature, and recently discovered substances are considered unpatentable.

Utility model applications may be organized and filed at local patent offices in countries where utility model protection is presented. On the other hand, an international patent application may be filed in a country belonging to the Patent Cooperation Treaty. Most countries, which recognize this treaty and have utility model laws, authorize utility model applications to continue as national phase applications of the international patent application. "The past 15 years have seen the introduction of utility model protection in at least 25 jurisdictions which did not have them previously. Whereas the early trend seems to have been to have different standards for novelty between patents and utility models, particularly in countries having an absolute novelty standard for patents, the current trend seems to be away from this and toward only requiring a reduced level of inventiveness for utility model protection" (Richards, John).

The United States Patent and Trademark Office first must determine if an invention is new. Once they determine it is, they decide if it is non-obvious. They present several questions in trying to determine this, such as: Would someone who was accomplished in the specific field of the invention believe it to be an astounding advancement? and, Do these same experts consider the invention to be unexpected?

There are many types of creative works that may qualify for a utility model patent: chemical formulas, processes or procedures, computer peripherals and hardware, software, cosmetics, biological inventions, electrical inventions, food inventions, housewares, machines, magic tricks, electronic circuits, medical accessories, medicines, musical instruments, odors, sporting goods, and mechanical inventions.

The application process in applying for a utility model patent is starts with filing an application with the USPTO, which is under the umbrella of the United States Department of Commerce. Second, the inventor may file what is known as a provisional patent application (PPA). This is for the purpose of obtaining an early filing date. Within one year of filing the PPA, the inventor must file a formal patent application complete with technical conventions, drawings, and words, to clearly instruct how to build and use the invention, give explanation of why and how the invention is unlike all previous and comparable developments (known legally as prior art), and accurately describe what aspects of the invention merit the patent or patent claims. The patent is then the focus of discussion between the inventor, applicant, and the United States Patent and Trademark Office examiner.

Industrial Design Rights Open Design

Industrial design rights are intellectual property rights that defend the visual design of objects that are not purely practical. An industrial design can be made up of the creation of a shape, configuration or composition of pattern or color, or combination of pattern and color in three-dimensional form containing artistic value. An industrial design can be a two- or three-dimensional pattern used to produce a product, industrial product, or handiwork.

United States design patents last 14 years from the date of grant and cover the ornamental aspects of serviceable objects. Objects that are deficient in a use beyond that granted by their appearance or the information they convey may be protected by copyright: a form of intellectual property of much longer length that exists as soon as a qualifying work is created. In some situations, rights may also be acquired in trade dress, but trade dress protection is akin to trademark rights and requires that the design have source significance or "secondary meaning." It is useful only to prevent source distortion; trade dress protection cannot be used to prevent others from challenging on the merits alone.

Open Design

Open design is the application of open source methods to the creation of physical products, machines, and systems. The principles of open design are a derivative of the Free Software and Open Source movements. In 1997 Eric S. Raymond, Tim O'Reilly, and Larry Augustin created "Open Source" as an alternative expression to "Free Software," and in 1997 Bruce Perens published the Open Source Definition. In late 1998, Dr. Sepehr Kiani, a Ph.D. in mechanical engineering from MIT, became conscious that designers could profit from Open Source policies, and in early 1999 he persuaded Dr. Ryan Vallance and Dr. Samir Nayfeh of the possible benefits of open design in machine design applications. Together they created the Open Design Foundation (ODF) as a non-profit corporation, and set out to develop an Open Design Definition.

Conclusion

"What you get by achieving your goals is not as important as what you become by achieving your goals."

Zig Ziglar

After you have completed the registration process, what are your next steps? That depends on your current dreams and goals.

In summation, it is imperative to comprehend that patents, trademarks, and copyrights constitute the basis on which fundamental intellectual property may be protected in law. It is therefore vital that a great degree of skill be exercised in drafting the documents and following the procedures required for obtaining this protection. By relying on a specialist in the field who has good standing and expert ability in his profession, the inventor or artist can be certain that their intellectual property will be sufficiently protected.

Trade Secrets

Once you have an idea, you may be enticed to protect your

creation by simply safekeeping its information and selling it to an enthusiastic buyer. The information is then known as a trade secret. A trade secret is a formula, practice, process, design, instrument, pattern, or compilation of information which is not generally known or reasonably ascertainable, by which a business can obtain an economic advantage over competitors or customers. In some jurisdictions, such secrets are referred to as "confidential information" or "classified information."

You will run into problems, however, if another person on their own initiative invents the matter of the trade secret. There is nothing to do to put a stop to that person from using it, applying for a patent, or publishing the information. A company can protect its confidential information through non-compete, non-disclosure contracts with its employees or within the constraints of employment law, including only restraint that is reasonable in geographic and time scope. The law of protection of confidential information effectively allows a perpetual monopoly in secret information. It does not expire as a patent would. The lack of formal protection, however, means that a third party is not prevented from independently duplicating and using the secret information once it is discovered. To acquire a patent, full information about the method or product has to be supplied to the patent bureau and, upon publication or issuance, will then be available to all. After expiration of the patent, competitors can copy the method or product legally.

Trade secrets are, by definition, *not* disclosed to the world at large. Instead, owners of trade secrets seek to keep their special knowledge out of the hands of competitors through a variety of civil and commercial means, not the least of which is the employment of non-disclosure agreements (NDA) and non-compete clauses. In exchange for the opportunity to be employed by the holder of secrets, a worker will sign an agreement not to reveal his prospective employer's proprietary information.

Companies often try to discover one another's trade secrets through lawful methods of reverse engineering on one hand and less lawful methods of industrial espionage on the other. Acts of industrial espionage are generally illegal under the relevant governing laws, such as if a trade secret is acquired by improper means.

Trade secrets have virtually no specific lifespan. As long as they remain secret, they can be trade secrets for eternity. There is, however, a risk associated with claiming a trade secret. With a trade secret, one is not allowed to claim copyright or patent rights. This means that if the secret becomes public, the creator will need to prove ownership of the trade secret.

Now get started on obtaining the protection your story, novel, invention, or creation deserves. We hope this book has been helpful in explaining to you the value of your intellectual property and the process or steps you will need to take in order to secure your rights and protect them, both for your peace of mind as well as a future of profits for you or your company.

Philo T. Farnsworth received the
first patent for a television in
1930.

Appendix

From the United States Patent Office

United States Patent	#6,812,392
Brando	November 2, 2004
Drumhead tensioning device and method	

ABSTRACT

In a tunable drum, a connector member in the drum is attached by linkages to a tuning ring, and is threadedly (sic) coupled by a tuning linkage to a retaining member fixed to the drum. Rotation of the tuning linkage with respect to the drum moves the connector member longitudinally and, as a result, adjusts the tension of the drumhead. In one embodiment, a motor is coupled to the tuning linkage such that an operator can manually adjust the tuning via a motor. In another embodiment, a transducer and tuning circuit can automatically provide control signals to the motor based on a difference between a desired frequency and a determined frequency.

Inventors:	Brando; Marlon (Beverly Hills, CA)
Assignee:	Penny Poke Farms, Ltd. (Beverly Hills, CA)
Appl. No.:	10/206,710
Filed:	July 25, 2002

RELATED U.S. PATENT DOCUMENTS			
Application Number	Filing Date	Patent Number	Issue Date <TD
133241	Apr., 2002	6667432	<TD
015489	Dec., 2001	6441286	<TD
878516	Jun., 2001	6410833	<TD

RELATED U.S. PATENT DOCUMENTS

Current U.S. Class:	**84/411R** ; 84/419; 84/454
Current International Class:	G10D 13/00 (20060101); G10D 13/02 (20060101); G10D 013/08 ()
Field of Search:	84/454,458,411R,419,413

REFERENCES CITED

U.S. PATENT DOCUMENTS

769527	September 1904	Bahr
1916123	June 1933	Greenleaf
3376777	April 1968	Becker-Ehmck
3701834	October 1972	Rubio
3747463	July 1973	Hinger
4023462	May 1977	Denov et al.
4112807	September 1978	Quibell
4122748	October 1978	May
4122749	October 1978	Hoellerich
4244265	January 1981	Tuttrup
4278003	July 1981	Hanson
4635524	January 1987	Allen et al.
4694726	September 1987	Silvestri
4709613	December 1987	Powers et al.
4741242	May 1988	Aronstein
4831912	May 1989	Allen et al.
4909125	March 1990	Fece
5157212	October 1992	Fleming
5392681	February 1995	Hall
5777248	July 1998	Campbell
5877444	March 1999	Hine et al.
5936179	August 1999	Merrick et al.
6043421	March 2000	Adams
6066790	May 2000	Freeland et al.
6291755	September 2001	Hine et al.

FOREIGN PATENT DOCUMENTS

592979	October 1947	GB

Primary Examiner: Donels; Jeffrey W

Attorney, Agent or Firm: Seed IP Law Group PLLC

PARENT CASE TEXT

CROSS-REFERENCE TO RELATED APPLICATIONS

This application is a continuation-in-part of application Ser. No. 10/133,241, filed Apr. 26, 2002, now U.S. Pat. No. 6,667,432, which is a continuation-in-part of application Ser. No. 10/015,489, filed Dec. 12, 2001, now U.S. Pat. No. 6,441,286, which is a continuation-in-part of application Ser. No. 09/878,516, filed Jun. 8, 2001 (now issued U.S. Pat. No. 6,410,833).

CLAIMS

What is claimed is:

1. A drum, comprising: a shell having a first mouth at a first end and a second mouth at a second end, the second end being opposite the first end along a radial axis of the shell; a drumhead covering the first mouth, the drumhead having a rim about its outer edge, the rim being positioned outside the shell; a tuning ring positioned over the drumhead, the tuning ring having an opening therein shaped to receive the first end of the shell and to prevent the rim from passing through the tuning ring; a plurality of elongated links having first and second ends, the first end of each of the links being coupled to the tuning ring, the links extending from the tuning ring into the shell through a plurality of holes in the shell; a connector member positioned inside the shell, the second end of each of the links being coupled to the connector member; a retaining member positioned within the shell on the side of the connector member toward the second end of the shell, the retaining member being coupled to the shell to remain longitudinally fixed with respect to the radial axis of the shell; a tuning linkage threadedly (sic) coupled between the retaining member and the connector member such that rotation of the tuning linkage moves the connector member longitudinally with respect to the radial axis and, as a result, adjusts the tension of the drumbead (sic); and a motor having a drive shaft selectively operable to rotatably (sic) drive the tuning linkage with respect to the retaining member to tune the drumbead (sic).

CLAIMS

2.   The drum of claim 1, further comprising: a user operable switch communicatively coupled to provide an actuation signal to the motor.

3.   The drum of claim 1, further comprising: a user operable switch communicatively coupled to provide an actuation signal to the motor, the user operable switch having at least three states including a first state in which the actuation signal causes the motor to rotate the drive shaft in a clockwise direction, a second state in which the actuation signal causes the motor to rotate the drive shaft in a counterclockwise direction and a third state in which the actuation signal causes the motor to not rotate the drive shaft.

4.   The drum of claim 1, further comprising: a transducer positionable (sic) to detect vibration of the drumhead, the transducer producing a vibratory output signal corresponding to at least a frequency of vibration of the drumbead (sic); and a tuning circuit having an input coupled to the transducer to receive the vibratory output signal from the transducer and having an output to supply an actuation signal proportional to a difference between a frequency of the vibratory input signal and a reference frequency.

5.   The drum of claim 1, further comprising: a transducer positionable (sic) to detect vibration of the drumhead, the transducer producing a vibratory output signal corresponding to at least a frequency of vibration of the drumbead (sic); a tuning circuit having an input coupled to the transducer to receive the vibratory output signal from the transducer and having an output to supply an actuation signal proportional to a difference between a frequency of the vibratory input signal and a reference frequency; and a motor controller having an input coupled to the output of the turning circuit to receive the actuation signal and having an output coupled to the motor to provide a motor control signal corresponding to the actuation signal.

6.   The drum of claim 1, further comprising: a transducer positionable (sic) to detect vibration of the drumhead, the transducer producing a vibratory output signal corresponding to at least a frequency of vibration of the drumbead (sic); a tuning circuit having an input coupled to the transducer to receive the vibratory output signal from the transducer and having an output to supply an actuation signal proportional to a difference between a frequency of the vibratory input signal and a reference frequency; and a user operable reference frequency input coupled to the tuning circuit to select the reference frequency for the tuning circuit.

CLAIMS

7. The drum of claim 1, further comprising: a transducer positionable (sic) to detect vibration of the drumhead, the transducer producing a vibratory output signal corresponding to at least a frequency of vibration of the drumhead; a tuning circuit having an input coupled to the transducer to receive the vibratory output signal from the transducer and having an output to supply a first actuation signal at a first time, the first actuation signal proportional to a difference between a frequency of the vibratory input signal and a reference frequency; and a user operable switch communicatively coupled to provide a second actuation signal at a second time, the user operable switch having at least three states including a first state in which the actuation signal causes the motor to rotate the drive shaft in a clockwise direction, a second state in which the actuation signal causes the motor to rotate the drive shaft in a counterclockwise direction and a third state in which the actuation signal causes the motor to not rotate the drive shaft; and a motor controller having an input coupled to the output of the turning circuit and to the user operable switch to receive the first actuation signal at the first time and the second actuation signal at the second time, the motor controller further having an output coupled to the motor to provide a series of motor control signals respectively corresponding to the first and the second actuation signals.

8. The drum of claim 1 wherein the motor is mounted at least partially within the shell.

9. A stand for retaining a drum and tuning a drumhead on the drum, the drum having a first coupling that is movable to adjust the tension of the drumhead, the stand comprising: a number of legs; a drum engagement member coupled to the legs, the drum engagement member dimensioned to supportingly (sic) engage at least a portion of the drum; a second coupling movably supported by the legs and dimensioned to detachably engage the first coupling of the drum when the drum is supportingly (sic) engaged by the drum engagement member; and a motor having a drive shaft drivingly coupled to the second coupling, the motor selectively operable to move the second coupling with respect to the legs.

10. The stand of claim 9 wherein the motor is selectively operable to move the second coupling with respect to the legs by rotatably (sic) driving the second coupling about a radial axis of the drum.

11. The stand of claim 9 wherein the motor is selectively operable to move the second coupling with respect to the legs by rotatably (sic) driving the second coupling about a radial axis of the drum and wherein the second coupling is

CLAIMS

selectively movable between an operative position in which the second coupling will engage the first coupling when the drum is retained by the stand, and an inoperative position in which the second coupling will not engage the first coupling when the drum is retained by the stand.

12. The stand of claim 9 wherein the second coupling projects upward when in an operative position such that lowering the drum into the stand when the second coupling is in the operative position will result in engagement between the first and second couplings.

13. The stand of claim 9 wherein the second coupling is pivotable (sic) between an operative position and an inoperative position.

14. The stand of claim 9, further comprising: a user operable switch communicatively coupled to provide an actuation signal to the motor.

15. The stand of claim 9, further comprising: a user operable switch in the form of a foot pedal communicatively coupled to provide an actuation signal to the motor.

16. The stand of claim 9, further comprising: a transducer positioned to detect vibration of the drumhead when the drum is retained by the stand, the transducer producing a vibratory output signal corresponding to at least a frequency of vibration of the drumhead; and a tuning circuit having an input coupled to the transducer to receive the vibratory output signal from the transducer and having an output to supply an actuation signal proportional to a difference between a frequency of the vibratory input signal and a reference frequency.

17. The stand of claim 9, further comprising: a transducer positioned to detect vibration of the drumhead when the drum is retained by the stand, the transducer producing a vibratory output signal corresponding to at least a frequency of vibration of the drumhead; a tuning circuit having an input coupled to the transducer to receive the vibratory output signal from the transducer and having an output to supply an actuation signal proportional to a difference between a frequency of the vibratory input signal and a reference frequency; and a user operable reference frequency input coupled to the tuning circuit to select the reference frequency for the tuning circuit.

18. A tuning assembly for a drum having a drumhead retained thereon by a tuning ring, the tuning assembly comprising: a connector member sized and shaped to be positioned inside the drum, the connector member being attachable to the

CLAIMS

tuning ring by a plurality of linkages extending from the tuning ring into the drum such that longitudinal movement of the connector member with respect to the drum will change the tension of the drumhead; and a motor having a drive shaft coupled to the connector member, the motor selectively operable such that rotation of the drive shaft longitudinally moves the connector member with respect to the drum and, as a result, will adjust the tension of the drumbead (sic).

19. The tuning assembly of claim 18 wherein the drive shaft is directly connected to the connector member to rotate the connector member therewith.

20. The tuning assembly of claim 18, further comprising: a tuning linkage coupled to the drive shaft for rotation therewith and threadedly (sic) coupled to the connector member such that rotation of the tuning linkage longitudinally moves the connector member with respect to the drum.

21. The tuning assembly of claim 18, further comprising: a tuning linkage mounted for longitudinal translation with respect to a radial axis of the drum and fixed to the connector member to translate the connector member therewith; and a gear coupled to the drive shaft to rotate therewith, the gear capable of drivingly engaging a portion of the tuning linkage to transmit rotation of the drive shaft to the tuning linkage.

22. The tuning assembly of claim 18 wherein the motor is sized and shaped to be received at least partially inside the drum.

23. The tuning assembly of claim 18 wherein the motor is mounted to a stand configured to support the drum.

24. The tuning assembly of claim 18, further comprising: a tuning linkage coupled to transmit movement to the connector member; and a stand configured to support the drum and to which the motor is mounted, wherein the stand has a detachable coupling to selectively couple the motor to the tuning linkage when the drum is supported by the stand.

25. In combination a drum and a stand for retaining the drum, the drum having a shell and a drumhead retained thereon by a tuning ring, the combination comprising: a plurality of elongated links having first and second ends, the first end of each of the links being coupled to the tuning ring, the links extending from the tuning ring into the shell through a plurality of holes in the shell; a connector member positioned inside the shell, the second end of each of the links being coupled to

CLAIMS

the connector member; a first coupling received in the shell for movement with respect therewith and coupled to the connector for transmitting movement thereto; a motor mounted to the stand, the motor having a drive shaft; and a second coupling sized and dimensioned to drivingly engage the first coupling, the second coupling coupled to the drive shaft of the motor for being moved thereby.

26. The combination of claim 25, further comprising: a user operable switch communicatively coupled to provide an actuation signal to the motor.

27. The combination of claim 25, further comprising: a transducer positionable (sic) to detect vibration of the drumhead, the transducer producing a vibratory output signal corresponding to at least a frequency of vibration of the drumhead; and a tuning circuit having an input coupled to the transducer to receive the vibratory output signal from the transducer and having an output to supply an actuation signal proportional to a difference between a frequency of the vibratory input signal and a reference frequency.

28. The combination of claim 25, further comprising: a transducer positionable (sic) to detect vibration of the drumhead, the transducer producing a vibratory output signal corresponding to at least a frequency of vibration of the drumhead; a tuning circuit having an input coupled to the transducer to receive the vibratory output signal from the transducer and having an output to supply an actuation signal proportional to a difference between a frequency of the vibratory input signal and a reference frequency; and a motor controller having an input coupled to the output of the turning circuit to receive the actuation signal and having an output coupled to the motor to provide a motor control signal corresponding to the actuation signal.

29. The combination of claim 25, further comprising: a transducer positionable (sic) to detect vibration of the drumhead, the transducer producing a vibratory output signal corresponding to at least a frequency of vibration of the drumhead; a tuning circuit having an input coupled to the transducer to receive the vibratory output signal from the transducer and having an output to supply an actuation signal proportional to a difference between a frequency of the vibratory input signal and a reference frequency; and a user operable reference frequency input coupled to the tuning circuit to select the reference frequency for the tuning circuit.

DESCRIPTION

TECHNICAL FIELD

The present invention is directed toward percussion drums and, in particular, to apparatus, systems and methods for adjusting the tension of a drumhead.

BACKGROUND OF THE INVENTION

Percussion drums have been used for hundreds, if not thousands, of years to produce sounds either alone or in combination with other musical instruments. A typical drum has a hollow body or shell over which a drumhead is stretched. A typical drumhead is circular and terminates at its outer boundary at a rigid or substantially rigid rim. When the drumhead is placed over the mouth of the shell, the rim is positioned slightly outside of the shell. A tensioning ring is positioned over the rim and is attached to the shell to retain the drumhead in tension across the mouth.

The tensioning ring is commonly attached to the shell by a number of threaded rods that extend between the tensioning ring and brackets on the outer surface of the shell. Threaded nuts are tightened on the threaded rods to move the tensioning ring toward the brackets, thus tightening the drumhead. A typical drum has six or more of such threaded rods. Accordingly, adjusting the tension in the drumhead typically requires the tightening of six or more separate nuts.

A number of tuning mechanisms have been developed in the past to make tuning the drumhead easier. Most of these mechanisms are incorporated into kettle drums, such as that illustrated in U.S. Pat. No. 4,831,912 to Allen et al. Other mechanisms, such as those illustrated in U.S. Pat. No. 4,244,265 to Tuttrup (sic) and U.S. Pat. No. 4,909,125 to Fece, have been developed for other types of drums.

None of the devices known to the inventor provide a simple and affordable drumhead tuner that is at the same time accurate and reliable. The mechanisms illustrated in Allen et al. and Fece, for example, are elaborate and likely expensive to manufacture. Accordingly, although they may be appropriate for expensive drums of the type illustrated therein, they may be inappropriate for simpler and/or less expensive types of drums.

Further, the mechanisms illustrated in Fece and Tuttrup are both subject to inadvertent adjustments that may accidentally modify the tone of the drum. The Fece device may be accidentally rotated, which would result in the drumhead tension changing. Similarly, the cables extending along the outside of the shell of the Tuttrup device could be displaced by the drummer or a drum stand, or the jackscrew inadvertently impinged, to accidentally change the tone of the drum.

DESCRIPTION

It is therefore apparent that a need exists for a simple and inexpensive drum tuning device that is also accurate and reliable and not subject to inadvertent adjustments.

SUMMARY OF THE INVENTION

The present invention is directed toward a tunable drum for use with or without a drum stand. Embodiments of the invention allow an individual to quickly and reliably tune the drum either manually, by operating a motor, or automatically by way of a tuning circuit.

In one particular embodiment, the drum incorporates a shell, a drumhead, a tuning ring, an adjustment or tuning assembly and a motor to drive the tuning assembly. The shell has opposing first and second ends with a first mouth at the first end and a second mouth at the second end. The drumhead covers the first mouth, and is retained against the shell by the tuning ring. The tuning ring is held against the drumhead by a number of cords, cables or other elongated linkages. The cables extend from the tuning ring to the adjustment assembly through holes in the shell. The motor selective drives turning assembly in response to actuation signals. A user or operator may manually operate the motor, or a feedback mechanism employing a tuning circuit may automatically operate the motor based on a difference between a desired vibrational (sic) frequency of the drumhead and a determined vibration (sic) frequency of the drumhead.

In another embodiment, a stand for retaining and tuning a drum includes a number of legs, a drum engagement member coupled to the legs, the drum engagement member dimensioned to supportingly (sic) engage at least a portion of the drum, a second coupling movably supported by the legs and dimensioned to detachably engage a first coupling of the drum when the drum is supportingly (sic) engaged by the drum engagement member, and a motor having a drive shaft drivingly coupled to the second coupling, the motor selectively operable to move the second coupling with respect to the legs.

In still another embodiment, a tuning assembly for a drum includes a connector member sized and shaped to be positioned inside the drum, the connector member being attachable to the tuning ring by a plurality of linkages extending from the tuning ring into the drum such that longitudinal movement of the connector member with respect to the drum will change the tension of the drumhead, and a motor having a drive shaft coupled to the connector member, the motor selectively operable such that rotation of the drive shaft longitudinally moves the connector member with respect to the drum and, as a result, will adjust the tension of the drumhead.

DESCRIPTION

In still another embodiment, in combination a drum and a stand for retaining the drum include a plurality of elongated links having first and second ends, the first end of each of the links being coupled to the tuning ring, the links extending from the tuning ring into the shell through a plurality of holes in the shell, a connector member positioned inside the shell, the second end of each of the links being coupled to the connector member, a first coupling received in the shell for movement with respect therewith and coupled to the connector for transmitting movement thereto, a motor mounted to the stand, the motor having a drive shaft, and a second coupling sized and dimensioned to drivingly engage the first coupling, the second coupling coupled to the drive shaft of the motor for being moved thereby.

In yet a further embodiment, a method for tuning a drumhead on a drum includes determining an operational state for a motor based at least in part on a frequency of vibration of the drumhead and operating the motor in the determined operational state to vary a tension of the drumhead. Determining an operational state for a motor based at least in part on a frequency of vibration of the drumhead may include selecting a first operational state corresponding to a rotation of a drive shaft of the motor in a first direction if the frequency of vibration of the drumhead is above a first reference frequency level, selecting a second operational state corresponding to a rotation of the drive shaft of the motor in a second direction if the frequency of vibration of the drumhead is below a second reference frequency level, and selecting a third operational state corresponding to no rotation of the drive shaft of the motor if the frequency of vibration of the drumhead is between the first and the second reference frequency levels.

In still a further aspect a method for facilitating the tuning of a drum comprises extending a plurality of linkages from a tuning ring at an end of the drum to a connector member positioned inside the drum such that axial movement of the connector member results in axial movement of the tuning ring, coupling the connector member to a motor, and operating the motor such that rotation of a drive shaft of the motor results in axial movement of the connector member.

BRIEF DESCRIPTION OF THE DRAWINGS

FIG. 1 is an isometric view of a drum and a drum stand according to one particular embodiment of the present invention.

FIG. 2 is an isometric cutaway view of the drum and the drum stand of FIG. 1, illustrating a tuning assembly according to this particular embodiment of the present invention.

DESCRIPTION

FIG. 3 is a sectional elevation view of an upper portion of the drum of FIG. 2, seen along Section 3--3.

FIG. 4 is an elevation view of a lower portion of the drum of FIG. 2 illustrating the tuning assembly engaged with a portion of the drum stand of FIG. 2, shown with portions of the invention cut along a diametric section.

FIG. 5 is a plan view of a connector member in the form of a spider member of the tuning assembly of FIG. 4.

FIG. 6 is a sectional elevation view of the spider member of FIG. 5, seen along Section 6--6.

FIG. 7 is an isometric view of a lower portion of the tuning assembly of FIG. 4 and an actuator from the drum stand of FIG. 4.

FIG. 8 is an isometric view of an actuator of a drum stand according to another particular embodiment of the present invention, shown in an operative configuration.

FIG. 9 is an isometric view of the actuator of FIG. 8, shown in an inoperative configuration.

FIG. 10 is an elevation view of a lower portion of a drum and a tuning assembly according to another embodiment of the present invention, shown with portions of the drum cut along a diametric section.

FIG. 11 is a sectional elevation view of an upper portion of a drum according to another embodiment of the present invention.

FIG. 12 is a sectional elevation view of a lower portion of a drum according to another embodiment of the present invention.

FIG. 13 is a functional block diagram of a drumhead tensioning device having a motor, motor controller, user manual control input, user reference frequency input, transducer, and tuning circuit, according to a further illustrated embodiment of the present invention.

FIG. 14 is an isometric view of a drum and a drum stand according to one particular embodiment of the present invention employing at least some of the elements of FIG. 13 where the motor is mounted to the drum stand.

DESCRIPTION

FIG. 15 is an isometric view of a drum and a drum stand according to one particular embodiment of the present invention. employing at least some of the elements of FIG. 13 where the motor is mounted within the drum.

FIG. 16 is a partial front, top isometric view of a drive shaft, threaded rod and sleeve for securely coupling the threaded rod to the drive shaft.

FIG. 17 is a partial isometric view of an alternative tuning assembly according to one particular embodiment of the present invention for use with or without a motor.

DETAILED DESCRIPTION OF THE ILLUSTRATED EMBODIMENTS

The present detailed description is generally directed toward systems, apparatus and methods for reliably and accurately tuning a drumhead, and for preventing accidental adjustments to the drumhead's tension. Several embodiments of the invention allow an individual to tune the drumhead through manual control of a motor and/or through automatic control of the motor to achieve a desired frequency of vibration.

Many specific details of certain embodiments of the invention are set forth in the following description and in FIGS. 1-17 to provide a thorough understanding of such embodiments. One skilled in the art, however, will understand that the present invention may have additional embodiments, or may be practiced without several of the details described in the following description.

FIG. 1 generally illustrates a drum 12 and drum stand 14 according to one embodiment of the present invention. The drum 12 generally has a shell 16, a drumhead 18 and a tuning ring 20. The shell 16 in the illustrated embodiment is in the form of a conga drum. The inventor appreciates, and one of ordinary skill in the art will understand, that the present invention can apply to a wide variety of drum types. For simplicity purposes, however, the following disclosure is directed toward the illustrated conga drum version of the present invention.

The illustrated drum stand 14 has three legs 22 supporting an upper ring 24 that encircles and retains the drum shell 16 when the drum 12 is in the drum stand. The upper ring 24 can be padded to protect the surface of the shell 16, and can be coated with a surface treatment to prevent the shell from rotating with respect to the drum stand when the shell is fully seated therein.

FIG. 2 best illustrates a tuning assembly 26 within the drum 12 engaged with an

DESCRIPTION

actuator 28 on the drum stand 14. The tuning assembly 26 incorporates a connector member such as spider member 30, a threaded rod 32, and a retaining member 34. The connector member is denominated herein as a "spider" member 30 where the connector member has elongated arms, but may take other forms as discussed below. The spider member 30 is connected to the tuning ring 20 by a number of cables 36. Each cable 36 is coupled to the tuning ring 20 at a location outside the shell 16, extends through a hole 38 in the shell, and is coupled to the spider member 30 at a location inside the shell 16. As discussed in more detail below, the threaded rod 32 passes through the retaining member 34 before terminating at a key 40 at its lower end. In the illustrated embodiment, the key 40 is positioned above a bottom rim 42 of the shell 16 so the drum 12 can be set on a flat surface without the key impinging upon the flat surface. The retaining member 34 is fixed to the shell 16, as discussed in more detail below.

FIG. 3 illustrates the relationship between the drumhead 18, the tuning ring 20 and the cables 36 in this particular embodiment. The drumhead 18 is generally circular, and terminates at its outer edge at an enlarged rim or bead 44. The bead 44 is positioned slightly outside the shell 16 when the drumhead 18 is properly fitted on the shell. The tuning ring 20 is complementary in shape to the shell 16 to fit over the shell and contact the enlarged bead 44 along its entire perimeter. Thus, urging the tuning ring 20 downward results in an increased tension in the drumhead 18. An upper surface 46 of the tuning ring 20 is curved downward, and is smooth to allow an individual to comfortably play the drum. A lower surface 48 of the tuning ring 20 has a number of hairs of prongs 50 spaced about the perimeter of the tuning ring to align with the holes 38. Each prong 50 projects inward from the lower surface 48 and upward when configured for use. The pair of prongs 50 thus creates a fastener to which an elongated rod 52 at the upper end of the cable 36 can be retained. The cable 36 can be wrapped around the elongated rod 52, or can be attached by any other means generally understood in the art. As discussed above, the cables 36 extend downward from the tuning ring 20, through the openings 38 in the shell 16 to the tuning assembly (not shown).

FIG. 4 illustrates the tuning assembly 26 according to the present embodiment. The spider member 30 is suspended between the cables 36 and the threaded rod 32. A threaded distal end 54 of the threaded rod 32 engages a complementary threaded opening 56 in the spider member 30. Rotation of the spider member 30 with respect to the threaded rod 32 thus results in relative axial movement between the spider member and the threaded rod. As discussed in more detail below, this relative axial movement ultimately results in changing the tension of the drumhead 18. The lower ends of the cables 36 each terminate in an enlarged head 58 that is retained by the spider member 30.

DESCRIPTION

The retaining member 34 of the illustrated embodiment is in the form of a cross with an aperture 60 at the intersection of four legs 62. Each leg 62 terminates at its distal end in a threaded portion 64. An elongated nut 66 having internal threads 68 extends through the shell 16 and threadedly (sic) engages the threaded portion 64 of each leg 62. The outer end of the elongated nut 66 terminates in a bolt head 70. In the illustrated embodiment, a washer 72 and a decorative plate 74 are positioned between the bolt head 70 and the shell 16. The retaining member 34 is thus fixedly attached to the shell 16. The inventor appreciates as would one of ordinary skill in the art that many different variations can be made to this particular structure without deviating from the spirit of the invention.

The threaded rod 32 extends from the spider 30 through the retaining member 34, where an enlarged, annular shoulder 72 prevents the threaded rod from moving axially toward the upper end of the drum. A bearing 74 is positioned between the annular shoulder 72 and the retaining member 34 to allow the threaded rod 32 to rotate with respect to the retaining member with reduced friction. Because the retaining member 34 from moving axially upward prevents the threaded rod 32, when the threaded rod is rotated with respect to the spider member 30 the spider member moves downward toward the retaining member.

The inventor and one of ordinary skill in the art would appreciate that many various structures can be used to move a connector member such as the spider member 30 axially with respect to the threaded rod 32. For example, as illustrated in FIG. 10, a threaded rod 132 can be threadedly engaged with a retaining member 134 and a shoulder 172 at the extreme distal end of the threaded rod can be seated above a connector or spider member 130 such that rotation of the threaded rod with respect to the retaining member causes the threaded rod, and with it the spider member, to move axially. The inventor appreciates that still further variations can be made without deviating from the spirit of the invention.

FIGS. 5 and 6 further illustrate the spider member 30 of the present embodiment. In the illustrated embodiment, six arms 76 project outward, corresponding to the six cables (not shown). For situations where more or fewer cables are used, the spider member 30 would have a different number of arms 76 to correspond with the number of cables in such a situation. The arms 76 are spaced radically at roughly equal angles with respect to the other arms to evenly distribute the forces that the cables 36 exert on the spider member 30. Each arm 76 terminates at its distal end in a groove 78. The groove 78 is sufficiently wide to receive the length of a cable 36 (not shown), but sufficiently narrow to prevent the head 58 (not shown) at the lower end of the cable from passing through the spider member 30. As illustrated in FIG. 6, a bottom

DESCRIPTION

surface 80 is tapered to compensate for the angle of the cable 36 as it extends upward from the spider member 30 and outward toward the tuning rim 20 (not shown). The inventor appreciates that other variations or shapes can be used for the spider member 30 without deviating from the spirit of the present invention. For example, a disk-shaped plate with detents distributed about its perimeter could be used. Likewise, the spider member 30 need not be flat, but instead could be curved downward to provide additional strength and/or to obviate the need for the tapered bottom surface 80.

FIG. 7 better illustrates the key 40, and the actuator 28 of this particular embodiment. The key 40 is fixedly attached to the extreme bottom end of the threaded rod 32. In the illustrated embodiment, the key is in the shape of a Greek cross, although it is appreciated that any number of regular or irregular shapes (other than a circle) can be substituted therefore. The key 40 incorporates four engagement members 82 to facilitate rotating the threaded rod 32. The engagement members 82 are sized to allow an individual to manually rotate the threaded rod 32 in addition to allowing the individual to rotate the threaded rod using the drum stand. Accordingly, configurations for the key 40 that facilitate both manual and assisted rotation would be optimal.

The actuator 28 has a number of channels 84 therein configured to complement the engagement members 82 on the key 40. The channels 84 are open to the top to allow the key 40 to be lowered into the actuator 28 from above when the drum is placed in the stand. The actuator 28 is fixed to the drum stand 14 to prevent relative rotation between the actuator and the stand.

FIGS. 8 and 9 illustrate the operative and inoperative configurations, respectively, of another embodiment the actuator of 128. The actuator 128 is connected to the stand 114 by an upper linkage 186 and a lower linkage 188. A locking member 190 is positioned between the upper and lower linkages 186/188 to retain the linkages in axial alignment. In this configuration, i.e., the operating configuration, the actuator 128 is upright and positioned to receive the key (not shown) for tuning the drum.

In FIG. 9, the actuator 128 is in the inoperative configuration. In this configuration, the locking member 190 has moved from the locked position to the unlocked position, allowing the upper linkage 186 to move with respect to the lower linkage 188. In the illustrated embodiment, the upper linkage 186 is pivotally connected at a hinge 192 to the lower linkage 188. The locking member 190 is a sliding collar that, when moved upward, exposes the hinge 192 to allow the actuator 128 to move into the inoperative configuration. When the actuator 128 is moved into the operative configuration, the locking member 190 is able to slide downward over the hinge 192 until it contacts a

DESCRIPTION

raised section 194. When the locking member 192 has slid downward until it contacts the raised section 194, the locking member prevents the upper linkage 186 from pivoting with respect to the lower linkage 188, retaining the actuator 128 in the operative configuration. The inventor appreciates that other configurations can be used to perform the above function, and thus various alterations and modifications to this illustrated structure would not deviate from the spirit of the present invention.

FIG. 11 illustrates a tuning assembly 201 according to another embodiment of the present invention. In the illustrated embodiment a drumhead 218 is retained against a shell 216 by a tuning ring 220. The tuning assembly of this particular embodiment incorporates a fastener 203, a plurality of linkages 205, a connector member 207, and a threaded rod 232. The parts of the drum and tuning assembly are that are not discussed in detail below are similar or identical to the corresponding parts discussed above. Accordingly, the applicant does not describe these features again.

The fastener 203 is coupled between the tuning ring 220 and the linkage 205. In the illustrated embodiment, an upper end 209 of the fastener 203 is curved and extends through a complementary opening in the tuning ring 220. Similarly, a lower end 211 of the fastener 203 has an opening engaged with the linkage 205. The exact manner of attaching the fastener 203 to the tuning ring 220 and/or to the linkage 205 can vary dramatically without deviating from the spirit of the present invention. A cap or similar structure can be captivity engaged with the linkage 205 to prevent the fastener 203 from disengaging from the linkage.

The linkage 205 is pivotally mounted to the shell 216 by a bracket 215. The bracket is mounted to the shell 216 by screws or other suitable fasteners. The bracket 215 has a central opening 217 that aligns with openings 238 in the shell 216. A rod 219 extends generally laterally across the opening 217 in the bracket 215, and serves as a fulcrum about which the linkage 205 can pivot during operation. The rod 219 can be integral with the bracket 215, or can be affixed or otherwise engaged therewith in any suitable manner.

The linkage 205 is contoured to pivot about the rod 219 during operation. In the illustrated embodiment, a ring 221 is formed along the length of the linkage 205, and encircles the rod 219. Because as discussed below the linkage 205 will be urged upward during operation, the upper portion of the ring 221 can be slotted or removed to facilitate engagement of the linkage 205 with the rod 219. The linkage 205 projects a relatively short distance outside of the shell 216, and projects inwardly toward a center line of the shell. Because the length of the portion internal to the drum is significantly greater than the length external to the drum, the force necessary to move the internal end of the linkage 205 is substantially lower than the resultant

DESCRIPTION

force generated by the external portion of the linkage.

Each of the linkages 205 engages the connector member 207. In a manner similar to the described above, the connector member moves longitudinally during operation in order to tune the drum. Consequently, the linkages 205 are coupled to the connector member 207 in a manner that allows for relative rotation between the two. In the illustrated embodiment, the linkage 205 rests in a complementary recess 223 that retains the linkage in the proper radial alignment during operation. The inventor appreciates that the linkages can be coupled to the connector member in a wide variety of ways without deviating from the spirit of the present invention.

The threaded rod 232 is engaged to rotate with respect to the connector member 207. In the illustrated embodiment, the threaded rod 232 is seated within an annular depression centrally located in the bottom of the connector member 207. A lower portion of the threaded rod (not shown) can be engaged with a structural member as discussed above to threadedly move in a longitudinal direction with respect to the shell 216. When the threaded rod 232 moves longitudinally, the connector member 207 moves as well. The inventor appreciates, however, that the threaded rod 232 can instead by threadedly engaged with the connector member 207 such that rotation of the threaded rod results in translation of the connector member. Consequently, the relative movements of the threaded rod 232 and the connector member 207 function similar or identical to those described above.

During operation, the user can rotate the threaded rod 232 to move the threaded rod and the connector member 207 longitudinally within the shell 216. When the connector member 207 moves up or down as oriented in FIG. 11, the external portion of the linkage 205 moves in the opposite direction. As a result, when the connector member 207 moves upward the external portion of the linkage 205 moves downward and the drumhead 218 is tightened. Because the length of the portion of the linkage 205 internal to the drum is substantially greater than the length of the linkage external to the drum, the amount of force required to move the connector member is substantially less than the resulting force exerted by the linkage 205 on the fastener 203 and, in turn, drumhead 218.

Embodiments of the present invention have numerous advantages over devices of the prior art. For example, because the key is manipulability (sic) both by hand and with the drum stand, the invention allows an individual to conveniently tune the invention both with and without the drum stand, and allows an individual to easily remove the drum from the drum stand to prevent accidental changes to the tension of the drumhead. To further prevent accidental changes, the cables extending from the tuning ring to the tuning assembly of the present invention extend almost entirely

DESCRIPTION

inside the drum shell. Thus, the drummer's hands, knees or the drum stand will not accidentally contact the cables, putting them in further tension and accidentally altering the tone of the drum.

Still further, because the actuator of the present invention is movable between operative and inoperative configurations, the drum can be left in the drum stand between uses and during use without the risk of accidentally changing the tension in the drumhead. Instead, the user merely moves the actuator into the inoperative position and uses the drum without worry that the tension of the drumhead will accidentally be changed.

Still further, because the tuning assembly is retained entirely within the boundaries of the shell, the drum can be set on the ground or otherwise carried and utilized without structural members getting in the way.

FIG. 12 illustrates another embodiment of the present invention. In the illustrated embodiment, threaded rod 332 is engaged to rotate with respect to the drum, as discussed above. The threaded rod 332 has a worm gear 333 fixed to it to rotate with the threaded rod during operation. The worm gear 333 has teeth 335 spaced around it, as is generally understood in the art. The teeth 335 on the worm gear 333 are enmeshed with a complementary thread 337 on a screw member 339.

The screw member 339 is oriented perpendicular to the worm gear 333, such that rotation of the screw member 339 results in rotation of the worm gear 333. The screw member 339 is fixed to a shaft 341 that extends across the internal cavity of the drum. One end of the shaft 341 is rotatably (sic) coupled to a bushing 343 in the shell of the drum, and the other end of the shaft extends through a similar bushing 345 on an opposing side of the shell. The shaft 341 projects beyond the shell, outside of the drum, and terminates in a handle 347.

During operation, the user can manually rotate the handle 347 to tune the drumhead. When rotated, the handle 347 causes the shaft 341 to rotate. When the shaft 341 rotates, the screw member 339 also rotates which, as discussed above, causes the worm gear 333 to rotate. When the worm gear 333 rotates, the threaded rod 332 rotates with it. As discussed above, when the threaded rot 332 rotates, the tension in the drumhead changes. Thus, when the handle 347 is turned, the drum is tuned.

FIGS. 13-17 show alternative embodiments of the present invention. In particular, FIGS. 13-16 show embodiments employing a motor, while FIG. 17 shows a tuning assembly 26 which may be driven by the illustrated motor, or may be driven manually as previously discussed. These alternatives will now be discussed with reference to

DESCRIPTION

the particular FIGS. 13-17.

FIG. 13 shows a motorized drum tuning system 401 for tensioning the drumhead 18 via the tuning assembly 26. The motorized drum tuning system 401 employs a motor 403 such as a servo motor having a drive shaft 405. The motor 403 is generally responsive to actuation signals 407a, 407b to turn the drive shaft 405 either clockwise or counterclockwise, or to stop or not turn the drive shaft 405. Thus, the motor 403 may have three operating states, clockwise rotation, counterclockwise rotation, and no rotation. As discussed in detail below, the drive shaft 405 of the motor 403 is coupled to, or is some embodiments forms a part of, the tuning assembly 26 to adjust the tension in the drumhead 18, for example by driving elements of the tuning assembly 26 such as the connector member (e.g., spider member 30, 130 and/or threaded rod 32, 132 (FIGS. 2, 4 and 10), connector member 207 and/or threaded rod 232 (FIG. 11), or threaded rod 332 and/or worm gear 333 (FIG. 12)).

The motorized drum tuning system 401 may optionally include a manual control input 409, allowing a user or operator to manually control the operation of the motor 403. The manual control input 409 can take the form of a switch or transducer having three switching states, corresponding to respective ones of the operating states of the motor 403. For example, the manual control input 409 may take the form of a "touch-sensitive" transducer, such as transducers that are responsive to skin or body characteristics for instance temperature (e.g., infrared sensitive), resistively , and/or chemistry. Also for example, the manual control input 409 may take the form of a touch-sensitive transducer responsive to an electrical ground supplied by the user touching the transducer 409. Some suitable touch-sensitive transducers are commercially available from Technical Solutions of Silvan, East of Melbourne, Australia.

The motorized drum turning system 401 may also optionally include a motor controller 411 for converting actuation signals 407a, 407b into motor control signals 413 suitable for controlling the operation of the motor 403. The structure and operation of motor controllers is generally known in the art of motor control.

The motorized drum tuning system 401 may also optionally include a transducer 415 and tuning circuit 417 for allowing the user or operator to automatically tension the drumhead 18 to tune the drum 12. The transducer 415 detects the vibration of the drumhead 18 as a vibratory input 419 and provides a vibratory output signal 421 to the tuning circuit 417, which is proportional to the frequency of vibration of the drumhead 18. The transducer 415 can take any of a variety of forms, for example a microphone to acoustically detect vibrations of the drumhead, a laser or other light source and receiver to optically detect vibrations of the drumhead, or a piezoelectric

DESCRIPTION

or other suitable tactile sensor to tactilely detect drumhead vibrations.

The tuning circuit 417 receives the vibratory output signal 421 at an input and compares the frequency of vibration of the drumhead 18 to at least one reference level representing a desired frequency of vibration of the drumhead 18. The desired frequency may be supplied by the user or operator via a user reference frequency input 423 as a reference signal 425, or may be predefined in the turning circuit 417. The user reference frequency input 423 may allow the user to enter any desired frequency or frequency range, or may allow the user to select between a number of predefined frequencies or frequency ranges. The user reference frequency input 423 may take the form of a switch, or may take the form of a sampler to acoustically sample a sound created by another drum or instrument. The tuning circuit 417 supplies an actuation signal 407b either directly to the motor 403, or indirectly via the motor controller 411.

The tuning circuit 417 may be implemented as a set of discrete electrical/electronic components and/or may be implemented as an integrated circuit such as a microprocessor, digital signal processor ("DPS"), or application specific integrated circuit ("ASIC"). U.S. Pat. No. 6,291,755 to Hine et al., U.S. Pat. No. 6,066,790 to Freeland et al., U.S. Pat. No. 5,936,179 to Merrick et al., U.S. Pat. No. 5,877,444 to Hine et al., and U.S. Pat. No. 5,777,248 to Campbell disclose various tuning circuits for stringed instruments. In operation, the tuning circuit 417 compares the determined vibratory frequency of drumhead 18 with a desired vibratory frequency. If the determined vibratory frequency of drumhead 18 is approximately equal to the desired vibratory frequency, the drum 12 is in tune, and no adjustment is necessary. If the determined vibratory frequency of drumhead 18 is not approximately equal to the desired vibratory frequency, the drum 12 is not in tune, and an adjustment is necessary. The tuning circuit 417 may employ a range around the desired vibratory frequency for determining whether the drum 12 is in tune. For example, the turning circuit 417 may compare the determined vibratory frequency to an upper and a lower reference frequency level, the upper and lower reference frequency levels being set some defined amount above, and below the desired frequency, respectively. The reference frequency levels should be set so as to prevent the feedback mechanism from unnecessarily oscillating about the desired frequency. The respective distances between the desired frequency and the upper and lower reference frequency levels may be not be equal in some embodiments, and may be equal in other embodiments.

FIG. 14 shows one illustrated embodiment of the motorized drum tuning system 401. The motor 403 and a printed circuit board 427 incorporating the tuning circuit 417 are enclosed in a housing 429, which is mounted to the drum stand 14. Power is provided

DESCRIPTION

via a common electrical cord and plug 431, or via batteries 433. The user manual control input 409 takes the form of a foot actuated pedal. The transducer 415 takes the form of a microphone mounted on the drum stand 14. Alternatively, the transducer 415 may be mounted on the housing 429. The drive shaft 405 of the motor 403 extends out of the housing 429 and is fixed to the actuator 28 to rotatably (sic) drive the actuator 28 in clockwise and counterclockwise directions. The actuator 28 selectively engages the key 40, for example when the drum 12 is received in the drum stand 14 to serve as a selectively detachable coupling. Operation of the motor 403 turns the actuator 28 and key 40 to selectively adjust the tension in the drumhead 18.

FIG. 15 shows another illustrated embodiment of the motorized drum tuning system 401. The motor 403 and printed circuit board 427 are received in the shell 16 of the drum 12. The transducer 415 may take the form of a microphone mounted on the printed circuit board 427. The transducer 415 may also take the form of a light source and receiver pair, mounted to the printed circuit board 427 so as to provide a clear optical path between the light source, the drumhead 18 and the light receiver. Thus, the light source may direct light to the drumhead 18, which reflects the light to the light receiver for detecting vibrations of the drumhead via time delay or phase shift methodologies. A reflective material may be employed on the inside surface of or as part of the drumhead 18 to increase the reflectance thereof. The transducer 415 may further take the form of a piezoelectric or other tactile sensor attached to inside surface of the drumhead 18. Alternatively, where the transducer 415 is a microphone, the transducer 415 may be mounted elsewhere, such as on the drum stand 14 or shell 16. In the embodiment of FIG. 15, the drive shaft 405 has a threaded end, and thus the drive shaft 405 serves as the threaded rod 32, 132, 232.

FIG. 16 shows a structure for coupling the drive shaft 405 to the threaded rod 32, 132, 232. The drive shaft 405 and threaded rod 32, 132, 232 have complimentary mating end portions 435, 437.

A sleeve 439, may positioned over the mating end portions 435, 437 to secure the coupling. (FIG. 16 shows sleeve 439 in a non-secured position to better illustrate the mating end portions 435, 437.) The coupling structure 435, 437, 439 of FIG. 16 may be employed with the embodiments of FIGS. 14 and/or 15.

FIG. 17 shows an alternative embodiment of the tuning assembly 26, which may be incorporated in the manual or motorized embodiments generally described above. FIG. 17 also illustrates the printed circuit board 427 in further detail.

The alternative embodiment of the tuning assembly 26 illustrated in FIG. 17 employs

DESCRIPTION

a linear rail or rack 441 to translate the connector member (e.g., spider member 30, 130, connector 207). The rail 441 includes a number of teeth for being drivingly engaged by a number of teeth on one or more gears 443 driven by the drive shaft 405 of the motor 403. The rack 441 may be employed with the other embodiments discussed above to realize the translation of the various actuating elements of those embodiments, such as the connector member 207 (FIG. 11).

The printed circuit board 427 includes the tuning circuit 417 implemented using a DSP 445 and a random access memory ("RAM") 447. The printed circuit board 427 also includes the motor controller 411. The motor 403 and the transducer 415 may also be mounted to the printed circuit board 427 to create a unitary package, allowing easy installation in the housing 429 (FIG. 14) or drum 12. The unitary package may allow for simple pre-market and/or aftermarket installation.

The inventor appreciates that the illustrated configuration is indeed merely illustrative. One of ordinary skill in the art, after reviewing the present disclosure, will appreciate that there are many equivalent means of transferring rotational movement from a first shaft to a second, unaligned shaft. In addition, the gear ratio between the two shafts can be adjusted to increase or decrease the torque transfer from the first shaft to the second shaft.

All of the above U.S. patents, U.S. patent application publications, U.S. patent applications, foreign patents, foreign patent applications and non-patent publications referred to in this specification and/or listed in the Application Data Sheet, are incorporated herein by reference, in their entirety.

From the foregoing it will be appreciated that, although specific embodiments of the invention have been described herein for purposes of illustration, various modifications may be made without deviating from the spirit and scope of the invention. Accordingly, the invention is not limited except as by the appended claims.

(Patent Courtesy the United States Patent and Trademark Office, **www.uspto.gov**)

Josephine Cochran received the patent for the dishwasher in 1886. She wanted a machine that could wash dishes quickly without breaking them.

Bibliography

About.com. (2008) A part of The New York Times Company.

Allman, Eric. Quote from **www.brainyquote.com.**

Aria, M.B. (2008) "A Brief History Of The U.S. Patent and Trademark Office," **http://www.best-business-skills-training-info.com**.

Bellis, Mary. (2008) "The First Federal Patent Act," **http://inventors.about.com/od/historypatentlaw/a/history.htm**.

Blackmoor, Brandon. (2007) "What is a 'shared universe'?" RPG Library.

Chander, Anupam and Madhavi Sunder. (2007) "Everyone's a Superhero: A Cultural Theory of 'Mary Sue' Fan Fiction as Fair Use." *California Law Review* 95: 597.

Copyright-protection-e.com.

Elias, Stephen and Richard Stim. (2004) *Patent, Copyright & Trademark: An Intellectual Desk Reference,* 7th Edition, Nolo/Delta Printing Solutions Inc., Berkeley, CA.

Harris, Tom. (2007) "How Patents Work," **http://www. howstuffworks.com/patent.htm**.

Heinze, William F. (2004-2007) "Creative Commons 'Attribution," **www.http://ip-updates.blogspot.com**.

Hollaar, Lee A. (2002) *Legal Protection of Digital Information*, BNA Books, Edison, NJ.

Information Technology Evaluation Services (1997) Public Schools of North Carolina.

Johnson, David. (2007) "Trademarks: A History of a Billion Dollar Industry" Information Please® Database © 2007 Pearson Education, Inc. All rights reserved.

Johnson, George. (2006) "A Brief History of Copyright Law."

Know, Tim. (2007) "Protect Your Ideas With Copyrights and Patents."

Kolsky, Alyssa. (2002) "Star Wars: Celebrities and Cybersquatting."

Larson, Aaron. (2003) "Fair Use Doctrine and Copyright Law," **www.expertlaw.com**.

Lundberg, Steven W. (2008) "Patents and the Internet," **www. slwip.com**.

Medill News Service.

Mott, Kelsey Martin. (2007) "The Concept of the Small Patent," in *The International Business Executive*, Volume 5, Issue 3, p. 23.

Nielsen Hayden, Patrick and Teresa Nielsen Hayden. (2006) "Fanfic: Force of Nature," *Making Light*.

Pressman, David and Richard Stim. (2006) *Nolo's Patents for Beginners*, 5th Edition, Nolo/Delta Printing Solutions, Inc., Berkeley, CA.

Pressman, David. (2006) *Patent It Yourself*, 12th Edition, Nolo/Consolidated Printers, Inc., Berkeley, CA.

Ralston, Rachel and Craig Fellenstein and Jaclyn Vassallo. (2005) "Patents, Copyrights, and Trademarks — A Look Back" from *The Inventor's Guide to Trademarks and Patents*, Prentice Hall.

Richards, John. (2002) "Petty Patent Protection" **http://www.ladas.com/Patents/PatentPractice/PettyPatents/PettyP01.html**.

Rogers, James L. (2003) *Protect Your Patent*, Sphinx Publishing, Naperville, IL.

Scott, Brian. (2007) "How to Copyright Your Music to Protect Your Future Profits and Royalties."

Stim, Richard. (2006) "Copyright Ownership and Rules," **www.researchcopyright.com**.

Stim, Richard. (2006) *Patent, Copyright & Trademark: An Intellectual Property Desk Reference*, 8th Edition, Nolo/Consolidated Printers, Inc., Berkeley, CA.

Stim, Richard. (2004) *Patent Pending in 24 Hours*, 3rd Edition, Nolo/Consolidated Printers, Inc., Berkeley, CA.

Suthersanen, U. (2001) "Incremental Inventions in Europe: A Legal and Economic Appraisal of Second Tier Patents," *in Journal of Business Law*.

Templeton, Brad. (2007) **http://www.templetons.com/brad/copyright.html**.

Thibadeau, Ph.D., Robert. (2004) "Thomas Jefferson and Intellectual Property including Copyrights and Patents," **http://rack1.ul.cs.cmu.edu/jefferson**.

Thomas, Paul. (2007) "How Copyright Protection Works."

Tushnet, R. (1997). "Legal Fictions: Copyright, Fan Fiction, and A New Common Law." *Loyola of Los Angeles Entertainment Law Review 17* (3): 651-686.

Tysver, Daniel A. "Copyright Licenses and Assignments," BitLaw.

United States Copyright Office. (2006) "Copyright Registration for Derivative Works."

United States Patent and Trademark Office, **http://www.uspto.gov**.

Vallance, Kiani and Nayfeh. (2001) "Open Design of Manufacturing Equipment," CIRP 1st Int. Conference on Agile.

Vallance, R. Ryan. (2000) "Bazaar Design of Nano and Micro Manufacturing Equipment."

Author Biography

Matthew L. Cole holds an M.A. in English, and spends most of his time reading, writing, or visiting local bookstores. He lives with his wife and son in Florida. He is the author of two novels, *The Widow Begley's Last Stand* and *Dead Horse Creek*. He has also written numerous articles, essays, short stories, and poems. This is his first book of nonfiction.

John Vincent Atanasoff's and Clifford Berry conceived the idea for the Atanasoff-Berry Computer (ABC) in 1937, and successfully tested it in 1942. The ABC is credited with being the first computer.

Index